DISCOVERING
MATHEMATICS

Investigations and Projects

BOOK 2

Nigel R. Peace

MACMILLAN
EDUCATION

For those who have guided me,
unknowing,
yet discovering

The author and publishers wish to thank the following who have kindly given permission for the use of copyright material: Dover Publications, Inc for material from *The Geometry of Life and Art* by M. Ghyka, Sheed and Ward (US), 1966 and Dover Publications, Inc New York, 1977.

Every effort has been made to trace all the copyright holders but if any have been inadvertently overlooked the publishers will be pleased to make the necessary arrangement at the first opportunity.

The author and publishers would like to thank Toby Glover and Alex Garland who drew the cartoons.

© N. R. Peace 1988

All rights reserved. No reproduction, copy or transmission of this publication may be made without written permission.

No paragraph of this publication may be reproduced, copied or transmitted save with written permission or in accordance with the provisions of the Copyright Act 1956 (as amended), or under the terms of any licence permitting limited copying issued by the Copyright Licensing Agency, 33–4 Alfred Place, London WC1E 7DP.

Any person who does any unauthorised act in relation to this publication may be liable to criminal prosecution and civil claims for damages.

First published 1988

Published by
MACMILLAN EDUCATION LTD
Houndmills, Basingstoke, Hampshire RG21 2XS
and London
Companies and representatives
throughout the world

Printed in Great Britain by
Richard Clay Ltd, Chichester, Sussex

British Library Cataloguing in Publication Data
Peace, Nigel
Discovering mathematics : investigations
and projects. —— (Discovering maths).
Book 2
1. Mathematics —— 1961 –
I. Title II. Series
510   QA39.2
ISBN 0–333–42297–X

CONTENTS

	Page
Preface	4
Index of mathematics topics	6
About this book	8

Investigations   **Topics covered**

1	How to write a book!	Logic, arithmetic, equations	11
2	Biorhythms	Arithmetic, graphs, frequency	19
3	Why count in tens?	Modular and base arithmetic	24
4	The progress of ideas	Biography, history of ideas	30
5	What are the chances...?	Sets, probability	33
6	Is it worth working?	Social arithmetic, money	37
7	Shop!	Money, probability	42
8	The long haul	Travel, speed, money	48
9	Measuring Britain	Maps, scale, angles	52
10	Measuring the world	Trigonometry, fractions, earth geometry, measures	62
11	Measuring yourself	Measurement, proportion	77
12	Loci and envelopes	Plane geometry, locus	81
13	Reshaping	Plane geometry, logic, trigonometry	86
14	Relations	Functions, logic	89
15	Multiple upon multiple	Arithmetic, algebraic proof	94
16	Squares and cubes and...	Factors, binomials, combination	99
17	Going off at a tangent!	Solution of equations, calculus	103
18	For the determined puzzler	Logic, frequency	106

PREFACE

There is a particular kind of school student – we all know one of them – who can be relied upon to ask at least once during each mathematics lesson: 'What are we doing this for? I mean, what use is it?'

Somehow the ready response: 'Because it's in the exam!', while of course true, seems less than satisfying to both parties. It might not be so bad if the same students didn't have a habit of coming back to visit you years after leaving school and loudly announcing: 'You know, I was right. I haven't used a fraction of the maths you taught me. Not a nought point one two fifth of it. Not in the *real* world.'

Is he right? Well, I think, only partly so. It is true that in the past there has been much deadweight in the syllabus and a reluctance to embrace new methods for fear, understandably, of jeopardising basic numeracy. Perhaps also many of us teachers have too often been unwilling to take the time and trouble (and, one might say, the opportunity) to examine critically our own courses and habitual practices. Because we have developed a love of the subject for its own sake perhaps we fail to realise that very few if any of our students have or indeed ever will have such a feeling – at least, not as long as we bore them rigid.

But on the other hand, mathematics *is* about the real world – its whole purpose is to enable us to understand the world better, to solve problems and communicate ideas. It is realistic not just by the knowledge it provides (the area of a circle, the slope of a hill, how many pounds make five) but also by the technique and method of it (algebraic analysis) which reflect and symbolise human reason.

So, yes, certainly most students will consciously use relatively little of the mathematical knowledge gained at school in later life – one rarely needs to know the area of a circle, and whether the gradient of a hill is 5/8 or 3/4 matters little when you're cycling up it. That's not the point though. Life certainly presents many opportunities for applying mathematical knowledge, if only one has developed that sort of curiosity. But even that isn't really the point.

What seems to be the most important point is that *every* student inevitably and in every moment of his or her life applies, to some degree, the technique and method of mathematics – in decision-making, problem-solving and judgements about number, size, shape, rate, relationship, probability, and so on. How successfully these methods work depends at least as much on the style of school maths as on one's 'natural ability'.

For surely the very best way to develop such success is not by sitting back in a classroom expecting maths to be delivered into one's head like so many bottles of milk, but by actually *doing* maths – by discovering. And if that mathematics can clearly be seen to be realistic, then not only is success more likely, it is also more likely that young people will develop a curiosity about and a care for maths that will last their whole lives.

I hope this book may provide some happy starting points for mathematical investigation and encourage students to develop their own projects.

N.R. Peace 1988

INDEX OF MATHEMATICS TOPICS

Topic	Most relevant investigations
Algebra: expressions, proof	15, 16
Angles	9, 10, 13
Area	10, 13, 16
Arithmetic	1, 2, 7, 15, 17
Base arithmetic	3
Binomials	16
Biography	4
Calculus	17
Circles	10, 12
Combinations	16
Computing	2, 7, 17
Earth geometry	10
Envelopes	12
Equations	1, 15, 17
Error, approximation	6, 8, 9, 10, 11
Factors	15, 16
Fractions: vulgar/decimal	9, 10, 11
Frequency	2, 18
Functions	14
Graphs	2, 17
History of ideas	4
Indices	10, 15, 16, 17
Locus	12
Logic	1, 13, 14, 18
Mappings	14
Maps	9, 10
Measurement	8, 9, 10, 11, 12
Modular arithmetic	3
Money	4, 6, 7, 8
Number systems	3, 4
Plane geometry	9, 11, 12, 13
Probability	5, 7
Proportion	11
Pythagoras	10
Rates and taxes	6
Ratio	9, 10
Scale	9
Set theory	5
Social arithmetic	6

Speed	8
Time	4, 8
Travel	8
Trigonometry	9, 10, 13
Volume	16

ABOUT THIS BOOK

The book is primarily intended for the 14 to 16 age group, but many younger students may also find projects here which are both interesting and rewarding. However, the investigations in this book, being directly linked to coursework leading to public examination, are usually rather longer and deeper than those of Book 1 whose projects are more of an introductory nature.

Many of the projects are divided into separate but related sections, which may be tackled alone or combined for more challenging work according to the student's experience. Several projects are also suitable for small groups of students working together. These factors should be a matter of discussion between student and teacher.

The sections are each labelled ●, ▲ or ■ as a very rough guide to their difficulty or the degree of previous experience required: ● requires only basic skills or knowledge to achieve worthwhile results, while ■ suggests that the project is really quite challenging either in its mathematical content or the degree of organisation required.

Very few students – or even teachers – are likely to have much experience in mathematical investigative work, and in any case one cannot lay down precise rules as to how such work must be carried out. Much depends upon the interests, personal style and perception of the individual; the important qualities are curiosity, care and sense of purpose. However, for the student to get the most out of the work, and to ensure that it can be properly assessed, some suggestions from Book 1 are repeated here:

1 The *title* and *purpose* of the work should be stated clearly at the beginning.
2 There should be a brief but clear description of the *methods* used, and a summary of any equipment necessary or books that were referred to.
3 All the information gathered, or calculations done, and so on, should be *recorded* neatly so that they can be understood by others.
4 Any *diagrams* should be neat and clearly labelled.

5 The *results* and *conclusions* should be fully recorded. (This is important whether or not the student thinks the results are 'good' or 'right'.)
6 There should be a brief but clear *summary* of the work. This should not only state what has been discovered but might also include some self-criticism or ideas for further work on the same themes.

A 'sample investigation' is included in Book 1 together with points of criticism for discussion.

How to write a book!   1

Most people enjoy puzzles and games, if only for fun; but if they can be educational too, so much the better. In this project you will see how to devise several popular maths and logic puzzles, and hopefully you can add some of your own ideas. You could make a booklet of them and give them to friends as an original birthday or Christmas present, or even sell them at school...!

● **PROJECT 1**

First, how is a booklet made? (The principle is the same for making newspapers.)

Take a sheet of paper and fold it (i) top edge to bottom edge, then (ii) left edge to right edge.

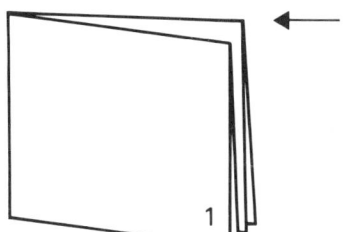

To make the booklet, this top edge would be trimmed off, but don't do this yet.

Now write the numbers 1 to 8 on each 'page' in turn, then open out the paper flat again.
Study the pattern of numbers.
Which numbers are 'back-to-back' to each other?
Which numbers are 'upside down'?

This shows how the pages must be arranged on a large 'master copy' sheet before the booklet is folded and trimmed.

Repeat the investigation for a booklet of 16 pages (four folds). Can you predict the arrangement for booklets with different numbers of pages?

PROJECT 2

Here are some ideas for maths and logic puzzles.

1 CROSS-EQUATIONS

Construct a grid, say, 5 by 5.
Blank out some squares and put in operation signs as shown.

Now put a number in each empty square so that every equation (there are six here) is correct. It will be more fair to the puzzler if you only use the digits 0–9.

Could there be any different arrangements of digits which also work in this grid? If you are sure there are no other possible arrangements, then copy the grid again without the numbers and the puzzle is ready.

But if there are other possible arrangements, how could you ensure that yours is the only 'correct solution' to the puzzle?

When you have got the hang of the puzzle, try making one with a larger grid and a different arrangement of operation signs.

For a more challenging puzzle you could include simple decimal numbers; in this case, you should give the positions of the decimal points in the grid.

2 LETTER CODES

Here is a puzzle that's easy to set but very hard indeed to solve. There are two versions.

(a) Write a simple 'sum' using words so that each letter stands for a digit. The words don't have to be mathematical.

```
  FIVE
+ FOUR
------
  NINE
```

Now decide on the value of each letter. Remember that a letter must always keep the same value, and each different letter should have a different value. In the example above, can you see that there is only one possible value for 'R'? What other restrictions can you see?

The puzzler now has to work out what value each letter must have for the sum to be correct. But again, are there any other correct solutions?

(b) Write some simple sums in equation form as shown. This isn't too easy! Now decide on a 'letter code' so that one letter will stand for one of the digits 0 – 9.

```
12 ×  7 =  84
 +    +    ÷
20 +  1 =  21
───────────
32 ÷  8 =   4
```

For example, let 0 = A, 1 = K, 2 = J, 3 = D, etc. Finally, rewrite the puzzle replacing each digit by its code letter.

Your victim has to work out the value of each letter so that all six sums are correct.

```
KJ × H = CB
 +   +    ÷
JA + K = JK
──────────
DJ ÷ C =  B
```

3 THE CRAZY TYPEWRITER PUZZLE

(a) Suppose an electric typewriter got its wires crossed and every time you wanted to type '5' it printed '3' instead.

```
  5 7 ×                          3 7 ×
    4                              4
  ─────      would appear as    ─────
  2 2 8                          2 2 8
  3 4 7 +                        3 4 7 +
  ─────                          ─────
  5 7 5                          3 7 3
```

Make up a sum like the one on the left so that there is a particular digit which appears several times in it. Now rewrite the sum, replacing that digit by a different one. The task is to identify which digit has been replaced.

Can you invent a sum which is still correct after a particular digit has been replaced?!

(b) The same kind of logic puzzle can be set using letters.

Write a short sentence. Then rewrite it, replacing, say, every 'e' with an 'f', every 'a' with a 'c', every 'i' with an 'n', etc.
Thus,

　　TAKE ME TO YOUR LEADER

will appear as

　　TCKF MF TP YPSR LFCDFR

The task is to work out the original message. This puzzle is extremely difficult to solve, so you should only replace a few letters, and then only replace them with letters which don't appear anywhere else in the message. You could also give a clue such as how many letters have been replaced.

HE WANTS US TO TAKE HIM TO OUR "LFCDFR"!?!

4　THE SEQUENCE PUZZLE

Here the puzzler is given patterns of numbers as clues, and he/she has to work out what the relationship is between the numbers in order to find a missing one.

For example,

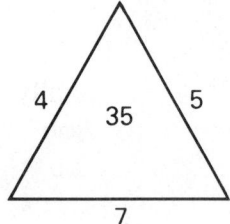 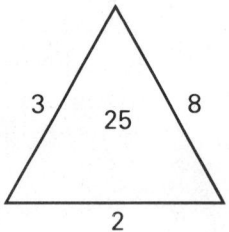 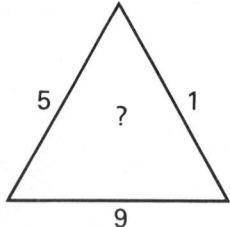

Of course, you decide in advance what the relationship between the numbers is to be. In this example the central number is the result of adding the left number to…! Could there be a different rule which works equally well?

In the puzzle above all the clues are quite separate, but it could be set so that the clues are related to each other.

For example,

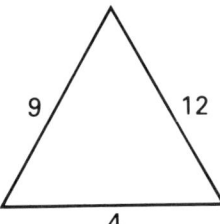 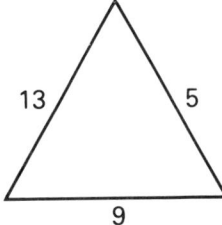 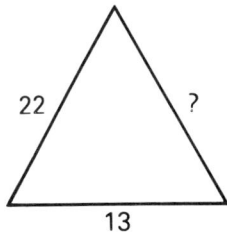

Here, the corresponding numbers on the first two triangles give the corresponding number on the last triangle....
But of course the puzzler does not know whether the clues are related or not!

A popular form of this puzzle is the 'number square'. In the example, reading left to right *or* top to bottom, the first two numbers are clues to the third.

4	5	13
11	??	32
19	20	58

5 EQUATION SEARCH

This is a popular puzzle, just like a wordsearch with numbers. The only drawback is that whoever sets it has to do just as much work as the puzzler!

Write a grid of numbers such as the one shown below. The task is to find as many hidden equations as possible, reading horizontally, vertically or diagonally. Bear this in mind when writing the grid so that you know there will be several quite difficult equations to be found. Even so, you're bound to find many more unintentional equations when the grid is finished, so check carefully!
You should know roughly how many equations there are to be found, so you can set a 'target' for the puzzlers.

5	7	12	9
14	10	2	18
20	3	2	3
7	4	28	30

Examples of equations in this grid:
 5 + 7 = 12   (top row)
 7 × 4 = 28   (bottom row)
 7 = 10 − 3   (second column)
 (5 + 10) × 2 = 30   (diagonal)
There are eight equations in this grid... I think!

6 CROSS-NUMBER PUZZLE

This is just like a crossword, except that all the answers are numbers; they fit in the grid one digit per square.

First make a grid so that the answers will be of several different lengths. It's best to make a fairly small grid at first until you're used to the method.

Next you have to label the starting point of each answer (using letters to avoid confusion with the answers themselves). Start at top left and work through the grid a row at a time, labelling every square where an answer could start (going across or down).

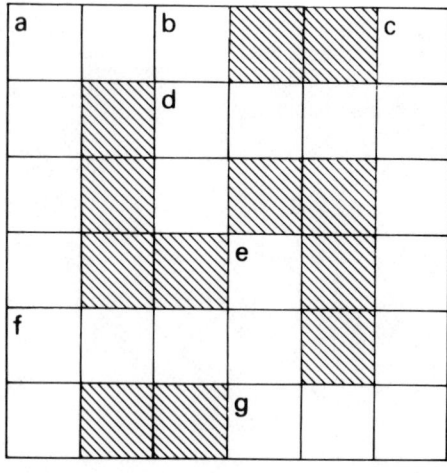

Now put a digit in each square, to form some interesting numbers – for example, dates, primes, palindromes, squares, etc.

The most interesting task is to invent clues for these numbers. They can be purely numerical:
 c Down   225 824 − 123 456
 f Across   248 + 275 × 10
Or the clues can be more 'cryptic':
 d Across   Two years after a World War.
 e Down   The hours in a long month.

Finally, copy the grid again without the numbers. It's a good idea to get someone else to check your answers before you set the puzzle!

7 NUMBER MAZE

This puzzle consists of a maze with *several* possible pathways from start to finish. Along the paths, and at junctions of paths, are written number operations.

First, carefully draw a maze of any shape so there are several alternative paths.

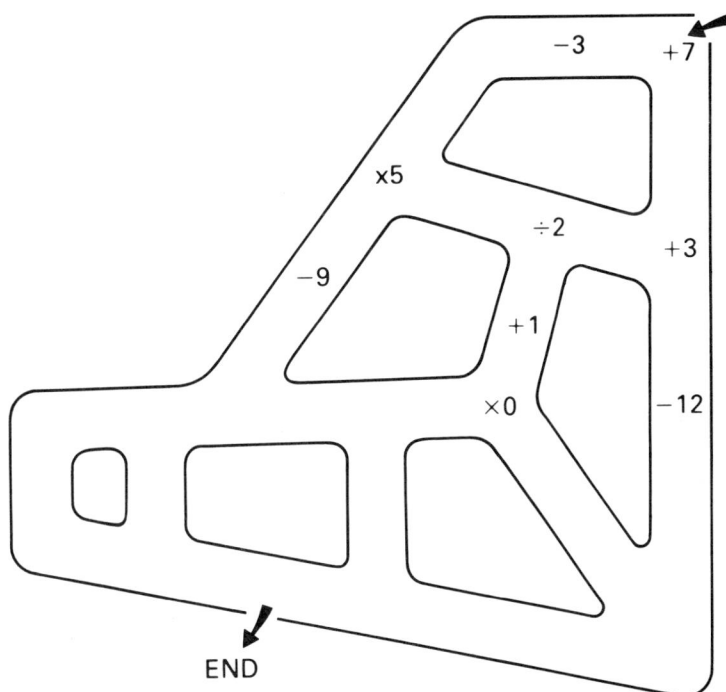

Possible tasks for the puzzler could be to find a path which gives the maximum total, or to find a path which gives a particular 'target' total which you specify, and so on.

You should keep the task in mind when you write in the number operations (just the first few have been shown in the example above).

Try to make sure there are a few paths with very similar, but not equal, results.

If the task is to find a target total, make sure that only one path gives it.

Why should you take special care in placing division operations?

8 THE FRENCH CROSSWORD

This puzzle is a crossword grid where words or numbers have to be fitted to the spaces. However, there are no clues! Instead, the answers are given – but there is only one way in which they can all be fitted into the grid. It is purely a test of logic.

Care and skill must be used in devising the grid itself, so start with a fairly small one. For the puzzle to be solvable you must ensure that there is only one possible position for one or two of the answers, and also that the answers are not too similar to each other.

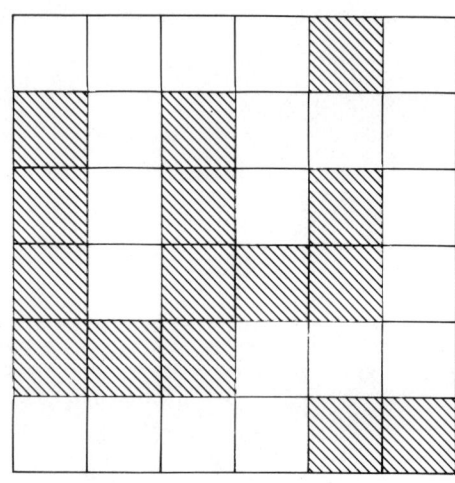

For the grid shown, check that there is only one possible position for a two-square answer and only one position for a five-square answer. However, there are three positions for three-square answers and three for four-square answers.

Next, write the answers to fit your grid using either numbers or words (numbers are easier). Check that there is only one possible arrangement for your answers before copying the grid out again and setting the puzzle.

The puzzle is more interesting with words that have something in common (say, names) or make a sentence.

For the grid above:

ALL MY MEN SLAIN, THIS VERY SAD HOUR!

There are further, more difficult, puzzles later in this book.

Biorhythms

2

● **PROJECT 1**

We are all familiar with many common cycles in life – events that occur regularly and with their own definite rhythm, such as the phases of the moon, the progression of seasons, the female menstrual cycle, and so on. Many people now believe that human beings experience other kinds of regular patterns, called 'biorhythms': this could be described as the ebb and flow of some sort of energy within us which affects our moods, health and alertness. If the theories are true, then knowing about these patterns should help us to predict 'critical days' ahead when we should be particularly careful (for example, when travelling) or days when we should be full of positive energy (for example, when taking exams!).

In this section you will investigate some of the theories of biorhythms and decide for yourself whether they are reasonable or not.

Note Although these theories are becoming very popular (you will be able to find several books about them in shops or libraries) they have not been proved.

There are supposed to be three main cycles:

Physical (repeating every 23 days): this represents the rise and fall of energy in the body

Mental (repeating every 28 days): representing the rise and fall of emotions and moods

Intellectual (repeating every 33 days): representing the rise and fall of our powers of reason, or memory.

These cycles can be shown on diagrams (called 'biograms') as waves. It is assumed that each cycle has

the same height and depth (called 'amplitude') and that each is divided into two equal halves, one 'positive' and one 'negative'.
Does this seem reasonable?
Where have you seen this sort of graph before?

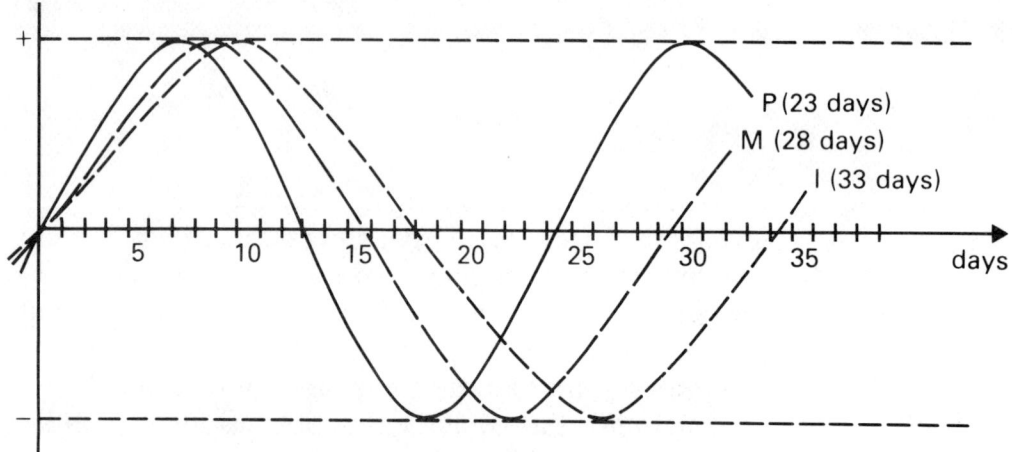

How to understand a biogram
- On days when the graph line is 'moving up', energy is increasing.
- Energy decreases as the graph line 'moves down'.
- 'Best' days are when a graph line is nearly at its peak (for example, around day 5 of the P cycle).
- 'Worst' days are when a graph line is nearly at its trough (for example, around day 20 of the M cycle).
- 'Critical' days, when one should be very careful, are when a graph line crosses the central axis from + to − or from − to + (for example, day 17 of the I cycle).
- 'Supercritical' days are when more than one of the three graph lines cross the axis at the same time!

You will need a calculator and graph paper.

(a) Calculate how many days you have been alive, including the day of your birth (and not forgetting leap years). Call this number N.
Divide N by 23 and study the 'remainder'.
How many days into the current 'physical cycle' are you?
When will your next 'physical cycle' start?

Repeat these steps for the 'mental cycle' (28 days) and the 'intellectual cycle' (33 days).

Mark in these dates along a horizontal axis on graph paper.

For each cycle work out the critical dates before and after the dates you have marked.

Also, work out the 'peak' and 'trough' days, and draw in the + and − lines (see example). Now sketch in the three waves, using a different colour for each.

Make a note of the dates which are 'critical' (and which cycle they relate to) or 'supercritical', and which dates are 'best' or 'worst' for each cycle.

Now put your biogram away, but keep a diary for two or three weeks making a note of any special events that have occurred – accidents, important meetings, successes or disasters at school, etc. – and how you reacted to them. Also make a note of days when you have had strong feelings – very depressed, or full of energy, rather ill, or on top of your form, etc. Then compare your diary with the predictions of your biogram, and decide whether there might be anything in these theories!

If you would like to take this investigation a little further, follow it up with one of these suggestions.

(b) Make a note of some important dates that are coming up in the future, such as exams, sports matches, meetings with someone special, and calculate your biorhythms for those dates. Do the biorhythms predict a successful day? If not, what could you do to make the day go better (to minimise the effect of 'low energy')?

▲ **(c)** It is thought that cycles can combine to form new cycles. For example, a combination of P and I produces a 'travel cycle' (what period would it have?). Perhaps it can predict good and bad days to make journeys. This might be useful for a nervous driver, or for someone who suffers with travel sickness! Draw up a travel biogram for someone you know who does a lot of travelling, and ask them to note down over two or three weeks any days when their journeys were particularly smooth or difficult. Then compare this information with your biogram's predictions.

(d) It has been assumed that biorhythms start from the date of one's birth, but is this reasonable? Should they perhaps start from the day of conception? If the average human gestation period is 294 days, what difference would this change in the theory make to the biograms you have calculated?

PROJECT 2

It would be useful to do some or all of the previous section before attempting this harder work. A calculator is all that is required, but this project could also provide the opportunity for writing interesting computer programs.

If the three main biorhythm cycles all begin simultaneously at birth, then every human being will experience the same 'critical days' at the same ages. This is difficult to believe since every individual is so different. Further, since the cycles all have different periods (not counting the different periods of 'combined' cycles), then 'critical days' must be quite frequent.

So the theory of biorhythms, however interesting, and even if actually true, might be pretty useless in helping someone to plan their life!

(a) Investigate how numerous and how frequent critical days are over an extended period of time. Start by analysing a single year, then an average lifespan of say seventy years. Remember that critical days occur at the end (or beginning) *and* the midpoint of each cycle.
For example, number of critical P days in a year is found by
    $(365 \div 23) \times 2$ or $365 \div 11\frac{1}{2}$.
Naturally, your answer must be an integer.

What is the average number of critical days per week?

How many 'supercritical' days are there in a given period of time, when two or three cycles coincide at zero?

How many more days are there when two or more cycles are simultaneously *within one day* of being critical i.e. days which are very nearly supercritical?

How many days are there in a average lifespan when all three cycles are restarting simultaneously?

(b) According to folklore, there are longer and more important rhythms in our lives – you have probably heard of 'the seven-year itch'. Also, the Bible often refers to '$3\frac{1}{2}$' as a significant time period, while many people believe there is a relationship between major world events and peaks of sunspot activity which occur roughly every $11\frac{1}{2}$ years.

By investigating the frequency of critical or supercritical days over an extended time, can you discover any periods when there are significantly more or less of these 'difficult' days?
If so, do these periods form any pattern?
If they do, does the pattern relate to any of the ideas described above?
(**Hint**   You might plot a graph of time against number of critical days per month....)

THE DEFENDANT PLEADS NOT GUILTY. APPARENTLY HIS BIORHYTHMS WERE ON AN "EXTREMELY VIOLENT CYCLE."

Why count in tens? **3**

● **PROJECT 1**

A **modular arithmetic** system starts with zero and contains a limited number of numbers, all integers. When the highest number is reached, for example in counting, you start again with zero. For this reason, modular systems can be represented on a 'clock' face.

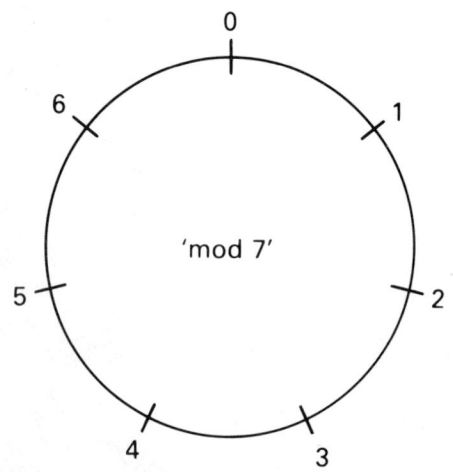

EXAMPLE
For addition, count clockwise; for subtraction, count anticlockwise. Multiplication is done by repeated additions, and division is...?
For example,
$$5 + 3 + 4 = 5$$
$$2 - 5 = 4$$
$$3 \times 5 = 1$$

(a) Investigate sums like these in other modular systems, for example, mod 5, mod 8, mod 12.
(b) Given a sum, can you find a way of working out which modular system it is in?
(c) Explain why an ordinary clock is a kind of modular system, and describe other ways in which we use modular arithmetic in everyday life.
(d) Modular 'clocks' can be used to draw geometric patterns (see below). Invent some designs of your own using other modular systems and rules.

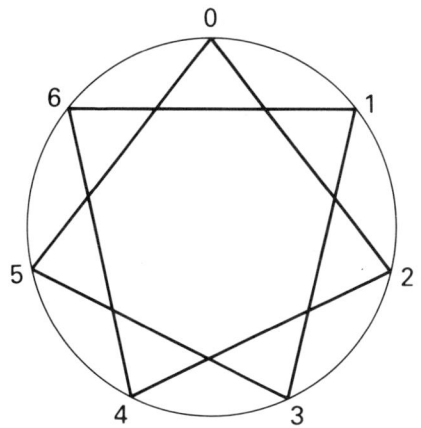

System: mod 7
Rule: $x \rightarrow x + 2$
(join each number to the number 2 greater).

(e) Some amusing limericks have been invented to describe modular arithmetic. Three of them are given below.
Can you invent some more?

There was a young fellow named Ben
Who could only count Modulo Ten.
He said: 'When I go
Past my last little toe,
I shall have to start over again.'

(Anon)

A lady of eighty, named Gertie,
Had a boyfriend of sixty, called Bertie.
She told him emphatically
That, viewed mathematically,
By Modulo Fifty she's thirty!

(J. McClellan)

A strange friend of mine, name of Shaw,
Used to sleep with a circular saw.
One day, in repose,
He lost one of his toes
And invented Mod Nine *and* Mod Four!

(N. Peace)

PROJECT 2

Here is a magic trick to make with which you will be able to tell the age of anyone up to 31.

First make five cards exactly like those below.

```
     Card A
  1   9  17  25
  3  11  19  27
  5  13  21  29
  7  15  23  31
```

```
     Card B
  2  10  18  26
  3  11  19  27
  6  14  22  30
  7  15  23  31
```

```
     Card C
  4  12  20  28
  5  13  21  29
  6  14  22  30
  7  15  23  31
```

```
     Card D
  8  12  24  28
  9  13  25  29
 10  14  26  30
 11  15  27  31
```

```
     Card E
 16  20  24  28
 17  21  25  29
 18  22  26  30
 19  23  27  31
```

Each card has the 'value' of the first number on it. Card A has value 1, Card D has value 8, etc.

Ask a friend to tell you on which cards his or her age appears, then simply add up the values of those cards. The answer will be your friend's age!

Now to investigate how the trick works.
(a) What have the values of the cards to do with binary arithmetic (base 2)?
(b) Show how *any* number between 1 and 31 can be written using only these values. For example,
   $3 = 1 + 2$, $11 = 1 + 2 + 8$, $25 = 1 + 8 + 16$.
(c) For each number 1 – 31, look which cards it appears on.
(d) Make a new set of cards to reveal ages up to 63!

PROJECT 3

The diagram on page 27 shows a method of coding information using 'punched' cards. For each column, a hole means 'yes' and a slot means 'no'.

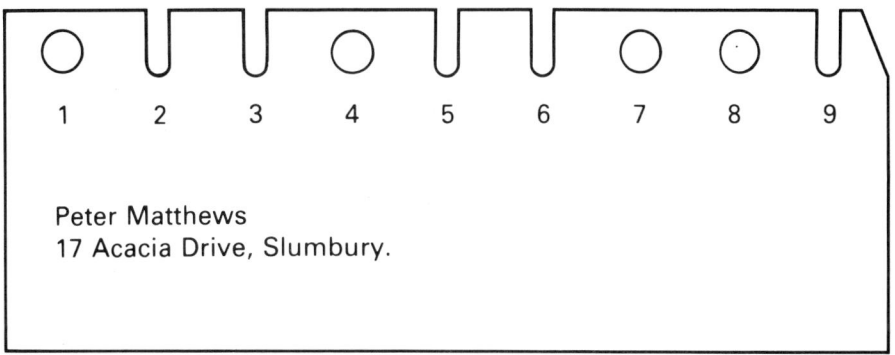

Peter Matthews
17 Acacia Drive, Slumbury.

Suppose that a card like this was made for each pupil in a school, and the numbered positions were given the meanings:
1 boy **2** girl **3** year 4 **4** year 5 **5** year L6
6 year 6 **7** mathematics **8** English **9** art

Can you see that Peter Matthews is a fifth year boy who is taking mathematics and English, but not art?
In this way, every pupil can be classified by age, sex, subjects or any other characteristic required. Then all the cards can be stored together in a box file for reference.

(a) What has this coding system to do with binary arithmetic (base 2)?
(b) Why has one corner of the card been cut off?
(c) What use are knitting needles in gaining access to the information stored on the cards? In particular, how can just the right cards be extracted for pupils who share several characteristics?
(d) Make up a set of cards for pupils in your class which code several pieces of information (such as age, sex, hair colour, favourite sport, method of travel to school, etc.).
(e) Can you devise other applications for this sort of system?

▲ **PROJECT 4**

How can a grocer weigh anything up to 100 g using only five kinds of weight?
Clue Base 3!

To investigate this, first show how any number between 1 and 100 can be expressed using just the numbers 1, 3, 9, 27 and 81. For example,
$5 = 9 - 3 - 1$
$20 = 27 + 3 - 9 - 1$

Now you must obtain or make a simple pair of scales and a set of 'base 3' weights. Use these to demonstrate how unknown weights may be found.
Some examples are shown below.

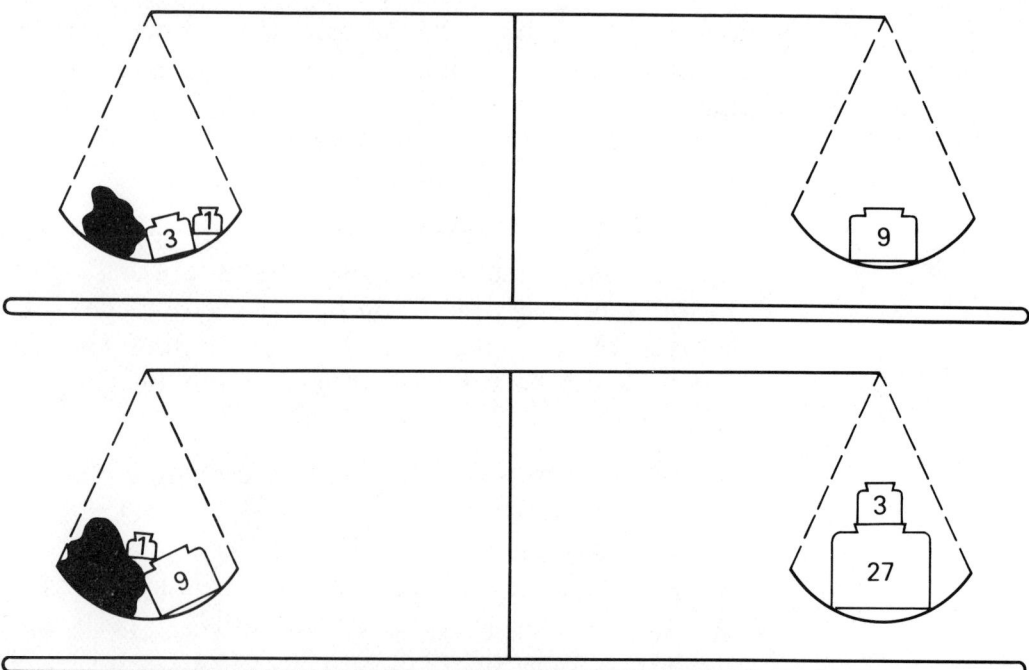

Are some weights easier to discover than others? For a simpler project you could use 'base 2' weights. But why is this method less useful?

▲ PROJECT 5

Here is an interesting method of coding which is extremely difficult to break, and for which you can devise many variations. It uses hexadecimal notation (base 16) in which the numbers 1 to 15 are represented by the digits 1 to 9, as normal, followed by the letters A to F (for example, 'D' means 13).

First you need to make a master grid of letters and numbers (they can be in any order).

A	B	C	D	E	F	G	H	I
J	K	L	M	N	O	P	Q	R
S	T	U	V	W	X	Y	Z	1
2	3	4	5	6	7	8	9	!

1	2	3	4
5	6	7	8
9	A	B	C
D	E	F	10

Secondly, make a rectangle of clear plastic big enough to cover a block of sixteen characters on the master grid, and mark it with sixteen equal rectangles. These are labelled with hexadecimal numbers as shown.

In how many positions can this decoder rectangle be placed over the master grid?

The first number in a piece of code represents the position to place the decoder. For example, 3 means line up the first column of the decoder rectangle with the third column of the master grid (CLU4).

The set of letters or numbers which follow the first number indicate the positions of the decoder which contain the message. A comma means shift to a new position. For example,

   COME AT 9   would be coded as   31863,11A,510

Note that there are many variations for the master grid and any character can be coded in many different ways; for example, in the grid above, 'T' could be coded as 1A or 29.

Try to improve on the example given, and develop your own coding system.

The progress of ideas   4

To understand a subject properly it is often useful to know something about how it has developed over a period of time: what the most significant ideas have been, how they came about (by chance, or because of some special need?) and what sort of people have contributed most.
Several areas of mathematics have fascinating history and you may like to investigate one or other of the following suggestions. Mostly, this will involve using libraries and asking librarians for help in finding information in the mathematics and history sections.

● **PROJECT 1**
   (a) Find out what sort of *number systems* and actual *numerals* have been used by different peoples in the past; try to describe how they worked, and which were the most successful.
   The most important systems to investigate are Ancient Chinese, Egyptian, Babylonian, Greek, Roman and Arabic.

   (b) Gather some information about famous *mathematicians* who have made important contributions to our knowledge. It will be interesting to know where and when they lived, what their important discoveries were and perhaps how old they were when they became famous. Try to discover whether there was any special feature about these people that made them great mathematicians.
   Here are twenty-three to get you started!
   Ahmes, Apollonius, Archimedes, Aristarchus, Aristotle, Cardano, Descartes, Diophantus, Einstein, Eratosthenes, Euclid, Gauss, Hipparchus, Kepler, Leibniz, Napier, Newton, Pacioli, Plato, Ptolemy, Pythagoras, Thales, Venn.

▲ PROJECT 2

(a) Progress in mathematics has often depended upon the ability to make longer and ever more complex calculations. The history of *calculating methods* is particularly fascinating: men have used simple everyday objects, ingenious paper-and-pencil methods, mechanical devices and then electric and electronic machines to take the hard work out of mathematics.

Investigate some of these methods and describe when and where they were first used, and some of their important advantages and/or disadvantages. Here are some ideas:
stones, tally sticks, the abacus, gelosia, Napier's bones, logarithms, the slide rule, mechanical calculators (look up Pascal and Leibniz in particular), the pocket electronic calculator and the computer.

(b) As old as calculating is the history of *money*, which is hardly a coincidence! The most important methods used in the exchange of goods and services have been barter, tokens, coins, precious stones and metals, paper money and credit (often called 'plastic money').

All of these are still used in different situations. You may like to describe examples of each one, for what purposes they are used, and their relative advantages or disadvantages.

Alternatively, you may prefer to concentrate on the development of one particular method, such as coins. What did the earliest coins look like and what were they made of? What different geometric shapes have been used for coins, and why? How are coins made nowadays?
To help with this research you could visit a coin dealer or look through coin catalogues.

PROJECT 3

As old as *time* itself is the measurement of it, for individuals and communities are generally more successful if they are organised and orderly. Agriculture and technology, in particular, both require the accurate measurement of time and men have developed ever more ingenious and precise *clocks*. The most important types of clock which you might investigate are:
sun, water, candle, sand, pendulum, gearwheel, electronic, quartz and atomic.
You should describe when and where they were developed, whether they had any special purpose, and how accurate they were.

By contrast, the development of *calendars* might seem pretty muddled. Since the Earth does not take an exact number of days to travel round the sun (and nor does the moon take an exact number of days to travel round the Earth), it is impossible to devise a perfectly accurate way of measuring a year. Many different systems have been used, and you might like to find out more about them: some really are quite extraordinary, while some of the more 'primitive' methods are actually more accurate than modern ones.
The most important calendars have been:
Assyrian, Aztec, Babylonian, Chinese, Gregorian, Hindu, Jewish, Julian (Roman), megalithic and Metonic (Greek).
For a speciality topic, you might like to investigate the method of calculating when *Easter Sunday* is to fall!

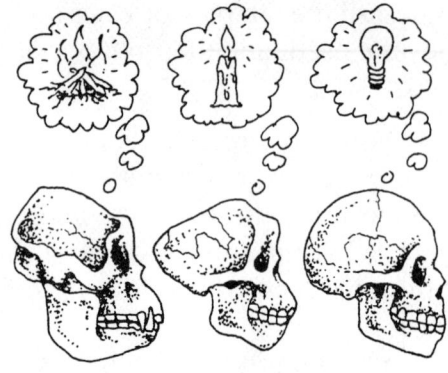

THE PROGRESS OF IDEAS.....

What are the chances...?

5

● PROJECT 1

On the next page is a game for you to make and investigate. But to prepare for that, try this puzzle first.

In the list below there are 13 symbols and 17 words. Can you arrange them *all* into ten groups of three, so that each group (or set) has something in common (the set 'characteristic')? Then, can you find a *different* arrangement using all the symbols and words?

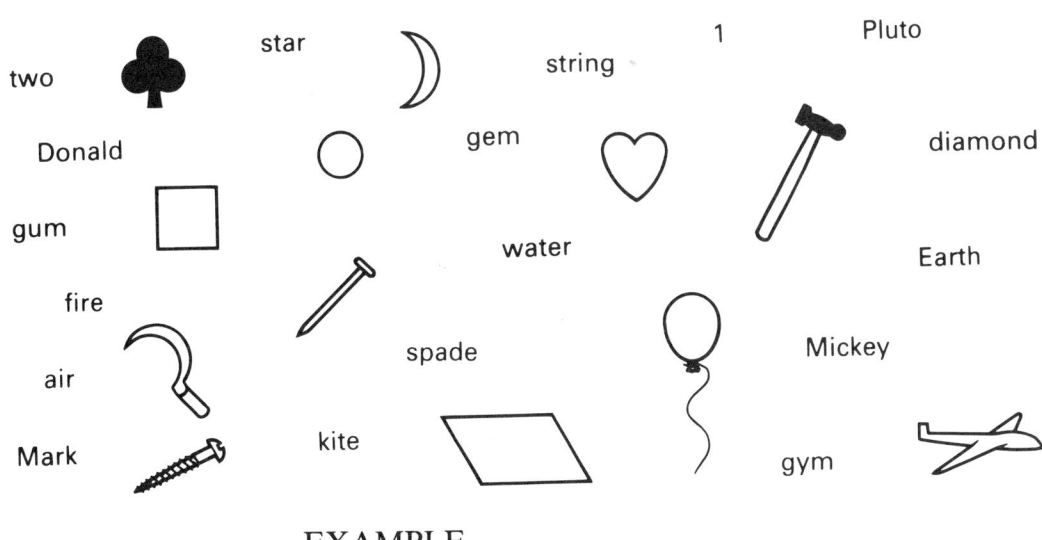

EXAMPLE
{ □, kite, ○ }
Characteristic: geometric shapes.
or,
{ diamond, ♣, spade }
Characteristic: playing card suits.

Try to find intersections between your sets.

Finally, take eight of your sets and try to rearrange them into six sets of four, or four sets of six.

34

▲ PROJECT 2

Suppose all the symbols and words in the previous section were on separate cards, placed in a box, and you were asked to pick one out blindfolded.
What is the probability that you would pick 'string'?
What is the probability that you would pick a symbol?
What is the probability that you would pick a name?
Check your answers with your teacher before going on.

Here is a game for several players which you can make.
You need a different counter or coin each, and one die.

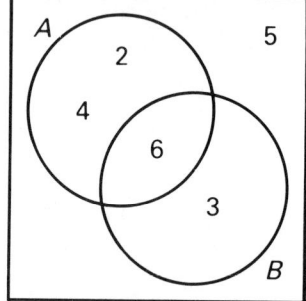

What is the significance of set A? Of set B? What about set $(A \cup B)'$?
The players put their counters on the board to show which set they hope will come up when the die is thrown – there are seven possible sets. The first player now throws the die, and everyone who was right scores the points shown below. (A '1' on the die scores minus 1 for the thrower!) Replace your counters before the next player throws the die; the winner is the first to score 20.

How to score
Before playing you should discuss (and explain in your account of the game)
(a) the meaning of the sets,
(b) how the probability is calculated, and
(c) how the score is calculated for each set.

Set	Characteristic	Probability	Score
$(A \cup B)'$	Divisible by 5	0.2	5.0
$A \cap B$		0.2	5.0
$A' \cap B$		0.2	5.0
$A \cap B'$		0.4	2.5
B	Multiples of 3	0.4	2.5
A	Multiples of 2	0.6	1.7
$A \cup B$		0.8	1.3

▲ PROJECT 3

Study the game in the last section carefully.
Now try to invent a similar sort of game, but more complex – some ideas are given below.
You should describe each possible set in symbols and words, and show how the probabilities and scores are calculated.

(a) For a larger version of the last game you could use three dice. The possible totals would be 3 to 18. There are many sets within these numbers: odd, even, multiples of 3, primes, squares, etc. When designing the board, try to make sure there are some intersections and some disjoint sets.

(b) Use a pack of playing cards instead of dice. Possible sets are: aces, clubs, red cards, court cards, and so on. Of course, there are many intersections between these sets.

You might design the board rather differently. One possibility is shown here: the lines between adjacent squares represent their intersections.

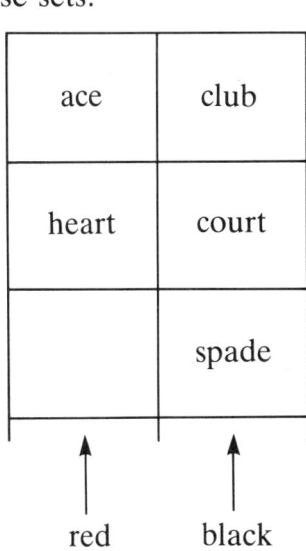

(c) Happy Families!

▲ PROJECT 4

There have been many famous experiments, especially at Duke University in the USA, which seem to suggest that telepathy – the ability to read someone else's mind – really does exist. In this investigation you can test it for yourself...!

Most experiments have consisted of card-guessing (you might be able to devise something more interesting, but keep it simple). For this you need to make five cards which are identical on one side; on the other side, each has a different picture or symbol which is easily recognised. These pictures should be *quite* different from each other, to avoid confusion. For example,

You might choose pictures of everyday objects (cat, moon, tree, etc.); it is thought that making them brightly coloured helps (why?).

Now, set up the experiment in a quiet room with a comfortable chair for your subject. One by one, you are going to look at a card for several seconds and ask the subject to write down which card he or she thinks it is. But note

(a) the order in which you choose the cards must be *random* – how could you ensure this?
(b) there must *not* be any possibility of the subject being able to see which card you choose!
(c) you should do a *long* run of guesses (at least fifty) with each subject – why? But then, why do you think a *very* long run is a bad idea?

Results

If you use five cards, the chance of guessing one correctly is $\frac{1}{5}$ or 20%. In a run of fifty, how many would you expect someone to get right if they are just guessing?
If a subject gets just a few more right than you might expect, it may be a fluke – repeat the experiment with them later.
But if someone gets *many* more right than they 'should', and is just as successful if the experiment is repeated, could they be using telepathy? *How* successful must someone be before we accept that telepathy is real? In other words, when is a fluke not a fluke…?

"JUST RELAX MR SMITH AND TELL ME THE FIRST THING THAT POPS INTO YOUR HEAD".

Is it worth working? 6

You have probably heard people complain, many times, that after paying tax, rates, rent or mortgage, gas and electricity bills, fares, etc., there is so little money left that it hardly seems worth earning! In this investigation you will try to discover if that is true. But first it would be useful to get to know more about the tax and rates systems.

▲ PROJECT 1

Tax is collected by the government to pay for national projects such as education, defence, the National Health Service, road-building, and so on. The important taxes that affect nearly everyone are VAT and Excise Duty (included in the price when you buy goods), and Income Tax.

How much income tax people pay depends on two things:

(a) their gross earnings, and
(b) their tax allowances.

- In 1986–7 the rate of tax was 29% for taxable income up to £17 200. Earnings between £17 201 and £20 200 were taxed at 40%, and there were higher rates for higher earnings.
- In 1986–7 the *single person's allowance* was £2335, the *married man's allowance* was £3655, and so on.

There are many other allowances which can be claimed. For any one person, the allowances are all added together and this total amount of earnings is *not* taxed.

EXAMPLE

A married man earns £24 500 and has total allowances of £4970. So his taxable income is £19 530.

The income tax he pays is:
$$\begin{aligned}&\text{£17 200 at 29\%} &= \text{£4988}\\&\text{£19 530} - \text{£17 200 at 40\%} &= \text{£ 932}\end{aligned}$$
$$\text{Total } \text{£5920 per annum}$$

Find out more about the system by writing to or, better, visiting your local Tax Office (look under 'Inland Revenue' in the telephone book). Ask questions like
- what are the present rates of tax, and the earnings to which they apply?
- what are the common allowances that people can claim?

Finally, invent some examples like the last one, and show how their income tax would be calculated. Perhaps you might choose a single person earning £9500 and claiming only a personal allowance, or a married man earning £31 000 and claiming allowances for the mortgage on his £40 000 house and for the £1560 he pays as maintenance to his previous wife....

▲ PROJECT 2

The local council of the area you live in also charges *rates* to every householder, to pay for local services, such as schools, refuse collection, housing, and so on. It is, in effect, a local tax.

Companies also pay this local tax, usually at a different percentage, and this money is called the *commercial rate*.

How much a householder pays in rates depends upon three things (note that for people who do not own their homes, the rates are often included in their rent):
(a) the *rateable value* of their home,
(b) the rate charged (a percentage of the rateable value, different for each local area), and
(c) any rebate or allowance they may be able to claim because of low income or a large family.

EXAMPLE

In 1986–7 the London Borough of Harrow charged a 'domestic rate' of 159.5%. A certain flat had a rateable value of £430 (no rebate claimed). Therefore the householder paid

1.595 × £430 = £685.85   per annum.

How does a Council fix the rate?

First it is decided how much money must be raised. The rate is this figure as a percentage of the total rateable value of all properties or companies in the area. More simply, the Council calculates how much can be raised by 1% (1p per £) of the total rateable value, and divides the amount required by this. For example, Harrow could raise £348 000 with a 1% rate in 1986–7. So a rate of 159.5% raised £55 506 000.

(**Note**   The council has other income as well, such as government grants, council house rents, and so on.)

Find out more by writing to, or visiting, your Local Council Finance Department. Ask questions like

- what are the present domestic and commercial rates?
- what are the total rateable values for your area?
- how much has your Council raised in rates this year (or how much is raised by a 1p rate)?
- how much income does the Council have from other sources?
- what are the most important things the Council *spends* the money on? What proportion is spent on these things?

Finally, try to visit your local Land Registry Office to find out what the rateable values are for some houses in your area.

Note   At the time of writing, important changes in the rating system are being planned.

■ PROJECT 3

There are many people who do not work, either because of personal circumstances or because they cannot find jobs. Most of these people receive help from the State – usually *unemployment benefit* or *supplementary benefit*. It is sometimes claimed that an individual might not even look for work because the state benefit they receive is more than they could earn. (Oddly enough, the same argument is used both by some unemployed people *and* by opponents of the benefit system!) Well, is this reasonable?

For this investigation it might be a good idea to share the work out in a group. You should invent two or three 'case studies' to consider, such as:

(i) A married man receiving unemployment benefit. He has been made redundant after earning £15 000 per annum. He has two children aged 2 and 6; the elder is at school and the younger is looked after at home by his mother. They live in a £40 000 house with three bedrooms which they are buying on a mortgage.

(ii) An unmarried woman receiving supplementary benefit. She has one child who is at nursery school all day. They live in a two-bedroomed council flat.

(iii) A school-leaver, living at home. He or she either receives supplementary benefit, or is on a government training scheme.

In each case, the question to be decided is: how much would this person have to earn in order to be better off financially than they are now with state benefit? (Clearly, you cannot take into account whether suitable work actually is available for these people.)

For each case study, present your findings carefully, showing income and important expenses for the two situations – employed or not. Try to decide on a figure for the minimum amount the person would have to earn to be better off working.

Your results might look something like the following (the figures are *not* accurate).
Victoria, single parent, one child, 2-bed council flat (case study **(ii)**).

Unemployed	£	*Employed**	£
Supplementary benefit	38.00	Rent	20.00
Heating all.	2.00	Rates	7.00
	——	Gas, elec.	8.00
	40.00	Nursery	10.00
Gas, elec.	8.00	Fares	10.00
	——	Prescriptions	1.00 av.
Amount left for living expenses	32.00	Living expenses	32.00 min.
		NI	12.00
		Subtotal	100.00
(All figures weekly)		Income tax $= \dfrac{29}{100}(52E - 2330) \div 52$	

* earnings are £*E* per week, with tax allowance of £2330 p.a.

$$\text{Thus}\quad \text{min.}\ E = 100.00 + \frac{29}{5200}(52E - 2330)$$

$$E = £122.55 \text{ per week or approx. £6400 p.a.}$$

Postscript
What other important considerations are there in deciding whether to work or not, apart from money?

Shop! 7

● **PROJECT 1**

This project is written in the form of a game for several players. Alternatively, one person can play alone trying to beat his or her own personal targets. Some ideas on how to develop the game and make it much more realistic are given in the next section.

Each player is the manager of a small cafe, buying fresh stock each day depending on what you think you can sell. Let's consider only five items at first – each player has a limited amount of money (your 'capital'), and a limited space to store his/her stock. Some items are perishable and have to be thrown away if unsold at the end of the day. How much a player actually sells depends on the weather, decided by dice!
At the end of each day, each player calculates his or her sales and profits (or losses), and decides what to order for the next day. The money available is the day's takings plus any of that player's original money not yet spent.
Then a player throws the dice to decide the next day's weather and each player works out how much he or she can sell of each item.
The winner is the player with most capital and stock after an agreed time, say seven days.

1 Stock
Here are some suggestions; these can be changed if desired.

Item	Cost price (p)	Selling price (p)	Profit on each sold (p)	Perishable
Tea (per cup)	10	25	15	no
Cola	12	25	13	no
Sandwich	18	46	28	yes
Cream cake	12	36	24	yes
Ice cream	8	24	16	no

2 How much can you buy?

This depends on how much money you have, and the space available. Let's say that each player starts with £50.00 to spend for Day 1, and the maximum amount he/she can store at a time is:

Tea	No limit
Cola	100 cans
Sandwiches	100
Cream cakes	30
Ice creams	100

3 How much can you sell?

This depends on the weather. If it is cold you will probably sell more cups of tea than if it is hot (but there may be fewer customers about!). In the chart below, two columns have been completed with suggested figures. You can decide how to fill in the rest.

Item	cold wet	warm wet	hot wet	cold cloud	warm cloud	hot cloud	cold dry	warm dry	hot dry
Tea	200	190							
Cola	50	60							
Sandwich	100	100							
Cream cake	20	22							
Ice cream	10	15							

4 What will the weather be?

For the first day throw two dice, one for rain and the other for sun.

		Result	
	1 or 2	3 or 4	5 or 6
Die 1	wet	cloud	dry
Die 2	cold	warm	hot

But the weather for tomorrow depends on today's weather – if it is wet today, it is more likely to be wet than dry tomorrow. So for the following days, throw the two dice and use the next chart.
(Study these charts and see if you can tell why they've been drawn as they are. Can you invent a better way of deciding the weather?)

Today	Result: die 1	Tomorrow	Today	Result: die 2	Tomorrow
wet	1,2,3	wet	cold	1,2,3	cold
	4,5	cloud		4,5	warm
	6	dry		6	hot
dry	1,2,3	dry	hot	1,2,3	hot
	4,5	cloud		4,5	warm
	6	wet		6	cold

(If today is cloudy or warm, the weather could turn either way, so use the dice as for Day 1.)

Now you're ready to play. Below is an example for one player who guessed that Day 1 would be warm but cloudy.

EXAMPLE

Order form

Day 1   **Capital at start of day:** £50.00   **Weather:** cold and wet!

Item	Brought forward	+ Order	= Stock	Demand	Sales	Profit (£)	Stock left	Loss on perishables
Tea	—	180	180	200	180	27.00	0	—
Cola	—	50	50	50	50	6.50	0	—
Sandwich	—	80	80	100	80	22.40	0	0.00
Cream cake	—	30	30	20	20	4.80	0	1.20
Ice cream	—	60	60	10	10	1.60	50	—
Value (£)	—	46.80	46.80		103.90	62.30	4.00	1.20

Capital available for tomorrow: £50.00 − £46.80 + £103.90 = £107.10

After Day 1 this player is worth £107.10 (capital) plus £4.00 (stock).

He/she could have sold more tea and sandwiches, but ordered too many cakes and ice creams – note that you can only sell the stock you have, even if the demand is higher!

▲ PROJECT 2

(a) The game in the last section could be made more realistic if you can get on good terms with one or two local cafe or shop owners and find out some actual prices, costs and sales figures. You could extend the range of items sold and investigate how other factors apart from the weather affect sales.

(b) You could use what you have learnt from the game to organise a small tuck shop at school, with profits going to your favourite charity! In what other ways could the ideas of this game be used to set up small local businesses?

(c) Potential stockbrokers and bankers among you might like to alter the game so that the items sold are shares or foreign currencies. Study the financial pages of national newspapers to decide what items to use and how their values change. You could invent a set of 'chance cards' for the game, describing political or commercial events which affect the value of shares, etc. (just as the weather affected cafe sales). Each player would start with, say, £1000 to invest and would try to maximise his/her profit in a given period of time.

You should also investigate how brokers use moving averages to predict changes in the market.

(d) The shop game also provides an excellent computing project in which the microprocessor is used to record and check stock levels, predict weather, and calculate profit, loss and capital remaining.

PROJECT 3

Many people buy goods by mail-order, choosing from a catalogue and usually spreading the payments over several weeks. Can you think of some advantages and disadvantages of shopping this way?

If you order goods for other people too you can earn 'commission', usually at 10% of the value of the orders if you take cash, or 12½% if you use the commission to buy more goods from the catalogue.

Below is a fictional catalogue and order form.

(a) Use these (or real catalogues if you can borrow them) to make up 'orders' for yourself, family and friends.
(b) Calculate how much commission you could earn.
(c) What could you buy using this commission? Make out a new order for this. But remember – this new order is earning you even more commission.
(d) How clever are you at using this system? Can you collect several 'orders', then order something for yourself so that the total commission you earn on *all* the orders exactly equals the price of the item you want for yourself? That way, you pay nothing!

Order form

To: Marsher Craigwood Mail Order Company					
Code C	Item	Size	Colour	Price	Weekly payment
....	....	....	....	....	....
....	....	....	....	....	....
....	....	....	....	....	....
....	....	....	....	....	....
(C = customer no.)			TOTALS		
Agent's name: Delivery address:			Commission due: Agent's number:		

Mail-order catalogue

Item	Code	Price (£)	Credit terms (20 weeks) (£)
Boy's shoes	BC 1	18.00	0.90
Trainers	BC 3	22.00	1.10
Socks (3 pr)	BC11	3.60	0.18
Jeans	BC19	16.99	0.85
Shirt	BC27	6.50	0.33
Tee-shirt	BC35	4.99	0.25
Jacket (denim)	BC54	26.99	1.35
Girl's shoes	GC 3	19.60	0.98
Boots (leather)	GC 6	24.99	1.25
Tights (pack of 3)	GC11	2.70	0.14
Jeans	GC19	16.99	0.85
Blouse	GC28	5.40	0.27
Tee-shirt	GC33	2.99	0.15
Dress (cotton)	GC43	10.20	0.51
Trouser suit	GC59	24.80	1.24
Jacket	GC67	21.50	1.08
Track suit	LC 8	17.20	0.86
Sports bag	LE 4	12.40	0.62
Tennis racquet	LE 9	17.50	0.88
Fishing rod	LE19	29.60	1.48
Ridge tent (2-man)	LE41	31.10	1.56
Sleeping bag	LE44	14.99	0.75
Touring bicycle	LE56	103.00	5.15
Portable radio	AE 5	7.99	0.40
Radio/cass. player	AE10	62.00	3.10
Portable TV (b/w)	AE31	99.50	4.98
Calculator	EE 7	12.60	0.63
Pocket camera	LE73	21.70	1.09

The long haul

8

● **PROJECT 1**

L London	A Amsterdam	BX Bordeaux
C Cherbourg	CL Cologne	M Madrid
B Boulogne	MC Munich	BA Barcelona
P Paris	G Geneva	R Rome

- - - motorway
.... normal road

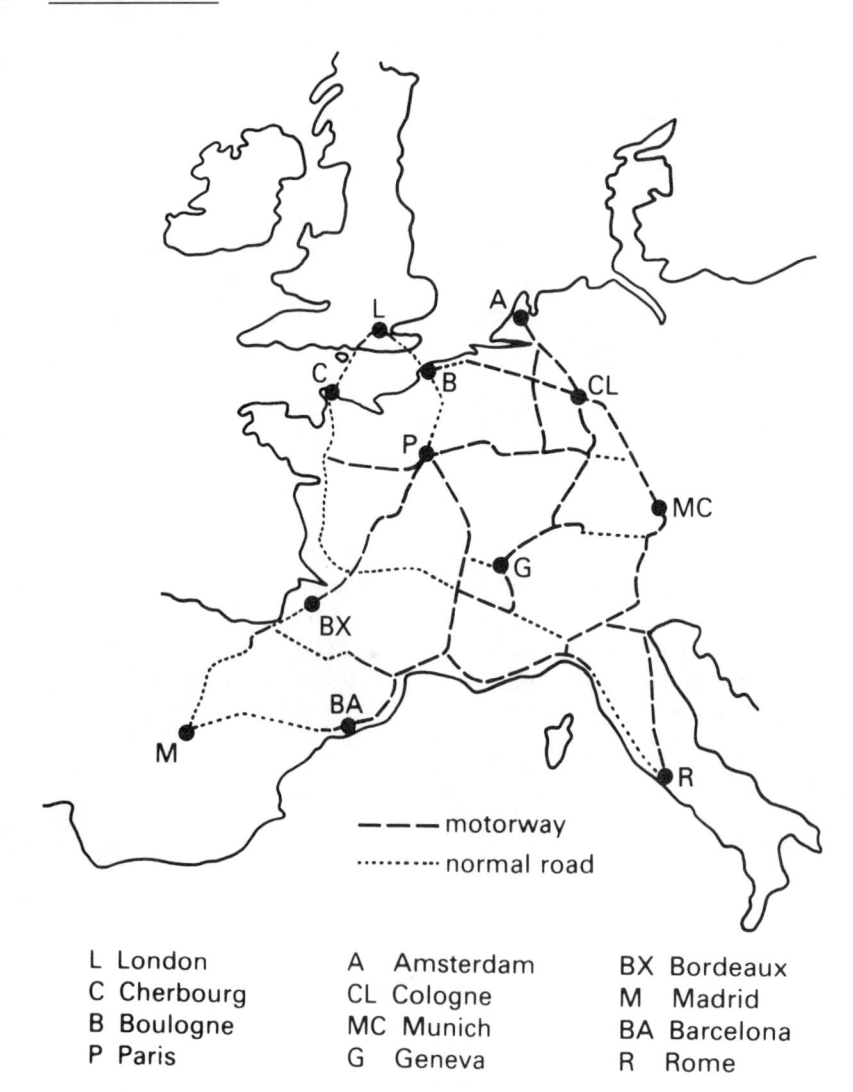

The map shows several European cities and the main routes between them. Opposite is a chart giving the distances in miles between these cities.

Distance chart (by road, in miles)

From \ To	B	P	BX	M	BA	A	CL	G	R	MC
Cherbourg	265	211	400	837	804	514	488	530	1115	721
Boulogne		161	504	942	803	245	268	476	1054	598
Paris			353	791	642	303	289	319	917	510
Bordeaux				438	404	656	658	438	991	796
Madrid					395	1094	1096	894	1303	1249
Barcelona						956	931	499	907	848
Amsterdam							162	572	1035	524
Cologne								437	930	362
Geneva									618	367
Rome										588

London to Boulogne
80 miles + 3 hours ferry/waiting time
London to Cherbourg
90 miles + 6 hours ferry/waiting time

Imagine you are a coach tour operator, driving people to several of these cities.
What must you take into account when planning the route?
What are reasonable average speeds to assume? (If a section of route is part motorway and part normal road you will have to estimate from the map the amount of each.)
(a) Choose three or four cities to visit, starting from London, and plan an itinerary. (You may need to use a more detailed map of Europe to plan overnight stops between major cities.)
(b) Plan a more complicated tour, showing different itineraries (visiting the cities in different orders). Describe the advantages or disadvantages of each.
(c) What is the shortest/fastest route by which you could visit *every* city shown on the map?!

▲ PROJECT 2

Investigate the road, railway or air network between the major cities in Great Britain.
Draw a map and a distance chart as in Project 1.
Plan tours to visit several cities.

If travelling by train, find out journey times from a British Rail Information Centre, and allow time for travel between station and hotel.
If travelling by air, find out flight times from a travel agency and allow time for travel between airport and hotel, for checking in and for baggage claim. What happens if a train or plane is delayed?

In Great Britain, how far could you travel and how many major cities could you visit in a week, travelling by air or train (or a combination of both)? Allow at least eight hours sleep a day – some of this could be on the train or plane!

▲ PROJECT 3

Choosing a summer holiday for the family can be quite a headache these days. Not only is there more choice than ever before, but to get the best deal possible means you have to study the holiday brochures very carefully indeed to compare prices and facilities. Sometimes there are 'special offers' to look out for. Some prices include VAT and some don't. What are the advantages of self-catering compared with 'full board' or 'half board'? What are the 'hidden costs', like travel?

Suppose you have to choose a holiday for a family of two adults and two children, aged 6 and 13. They live in London and have decided to go to a holiday camp where there is plenty of entertainment laid on, but they don't want to have to travel more than 200 miles (by car). They can go for one week, any time between the middle of July and the beginning of August.
Your task is first of all to go to a travel agency and collect several brochures (for example, Butlins, Pontin's, Warners, Ladbrokes or some smaller operators). Read them carefully then draw up an information chart to help the family with their choice.

In the example below only three possibilities have been compared.

Location/company	Travel	Facilities	Type of accom.	Food	Price 25/7	Total cost
Camber, Rye Pontin's	80 miles £24	Beach, kids' club, i/d pool, good sports, entertainment, TV, BMX, playground	chalet SC HB	£70 £30	£209 +VAT £370 + VAT	£335 £480
Beeson's, Torbay Ladbrokes	195 miles £58	Dartmoor, no beach, o/d pool, kids' club, good sports, etc., TV, archery (but some charges)	flat SC	£70 + elec.	£197 + VAT	£365 ?

Measuring Britain

9

● **PROJECT 1**

Many ancient sites in Britain – stone circles, burial grounds, churches, tracks – seem to lie along almost perfect straight lines, as if they had been deliberately planned that way. Such lines are called **leys**. Of course, alignments like this may be just coincidence. But they may suggest that our ancestors were more clever than we sometimes think, or that these paths and sites may have had special purposes which we know nothing about.

In this project you will investigate these ideas, using large-scale maps to try to find some leys (which may be quite short) and decide for yourself whether any you do find are significant or not. Ordinance Survey maps (1 : 50 000 or 1 : 25 000) are best; they can be bought at large bookshops or borrowed at some larger libraries. Choose any area of Britain that interests you.

Cover your chosen area with tracing paper and mark in pencil all the prehistoric sites, mounds, wells, tumuli, monuments, hilltops and churches (many churches are built on ancient religious sites).

Then draw straight lines between your marks, trying to line up as many as possible; you will probably be able to draw several lines with three or four sites on them.

It is also interesting to check the angles between these lines.

Examples are given on the next pages.
You will also find the book *The Old Straight Track* by Alfred Watkins very useful (published by Sphere Books). Finally, it might be interesting to measure distances not in metres or feet but in *megalithic yards* – an ancient land measure (1 MY = 2.721 feet = 82.94 cm).

EXAMPLE 1

This shows a few features of an area near Worthing in Sussex, where many similar alignments may be found. (Not drawn to scale.)

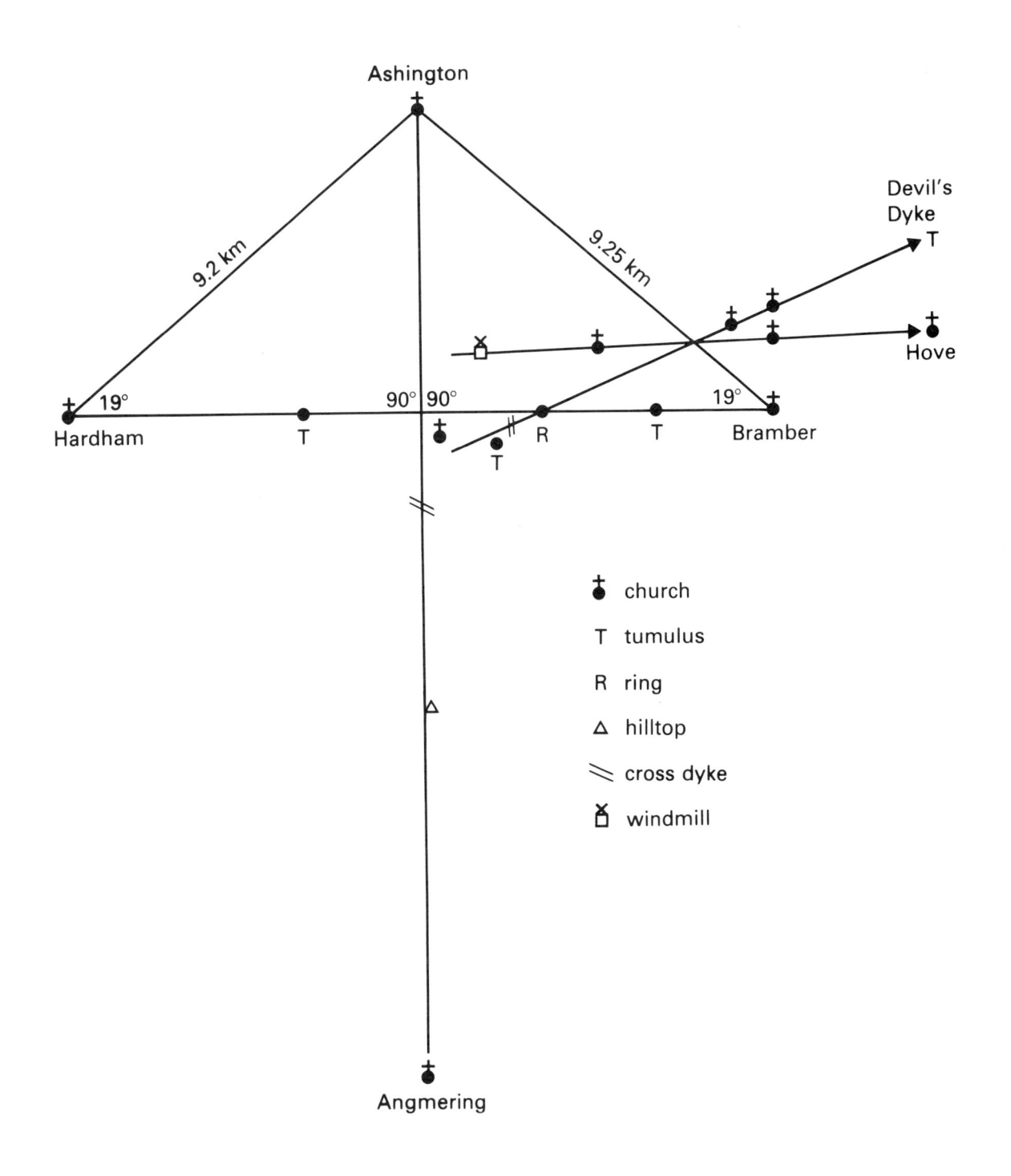

- ✚ church
- T tumulus
- R ring
- △ hilltop
- ⪤ cross dyke
- ⛉ windmill

EXAMPLE 2

Somerset and Wiltshire are also rich sources of ancient sites, the most famous centres being Stonehenge, Avebury, Wells and Glastonbury. The diagram below shows an area just north of Wells in Somerset.

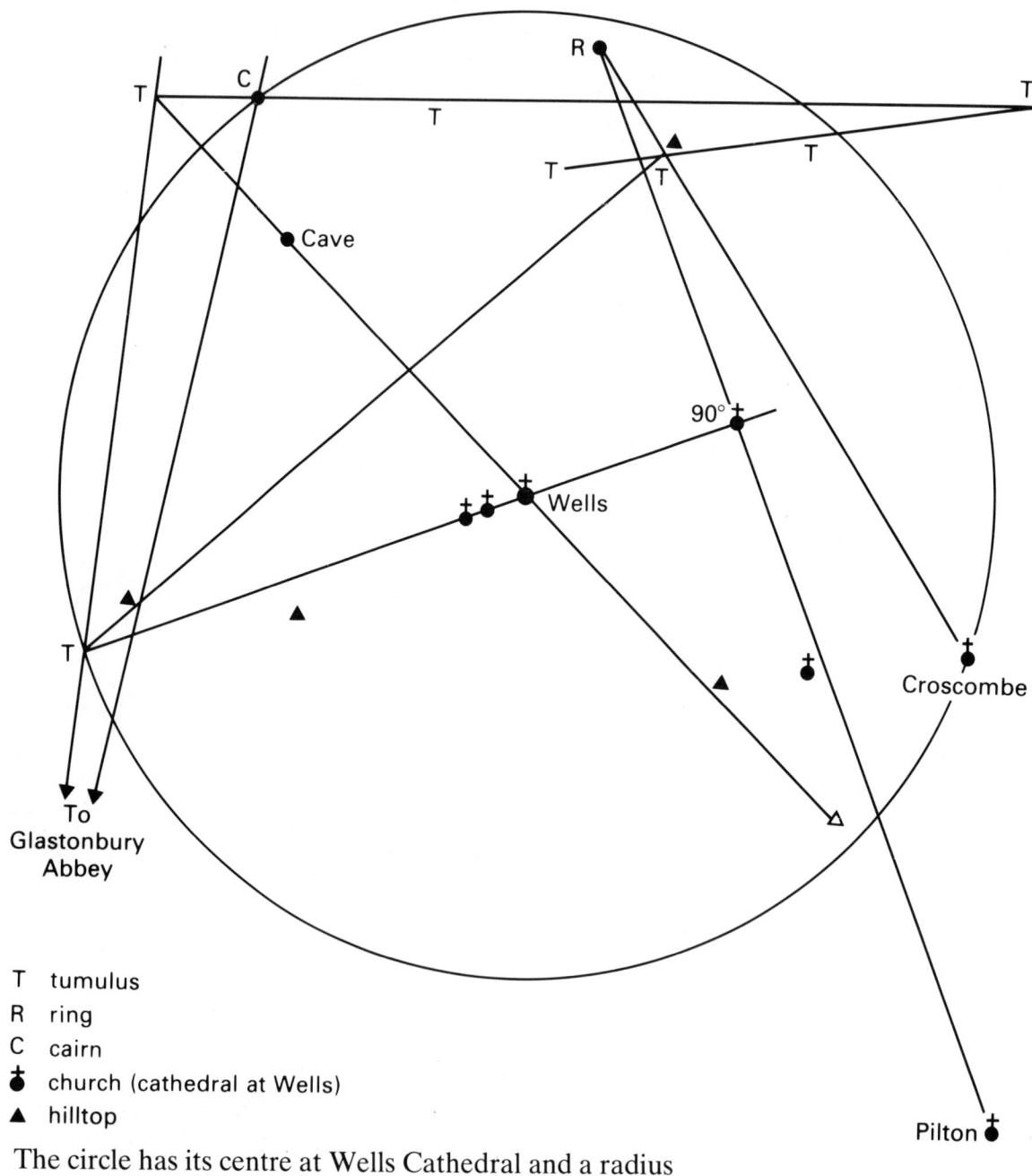

T tumulus
R ring
C cairn
⛨ church (cathedral at Wells)
▲ hilltop

The circle has its centre at Wells Cathedral and a radius of 4.1 km.

EXAMPLE 3

Glastonbury in Somerset is often said to be the centre of British Christianity. There are many ancient legends associated with the area and the ruined abbey is a very historic site (King Arthur is supposedly buried there!). The diagram below shows churches around Glastonbury in an arc centred on the abbey. (Not to scale, angles to the nearest degree.)

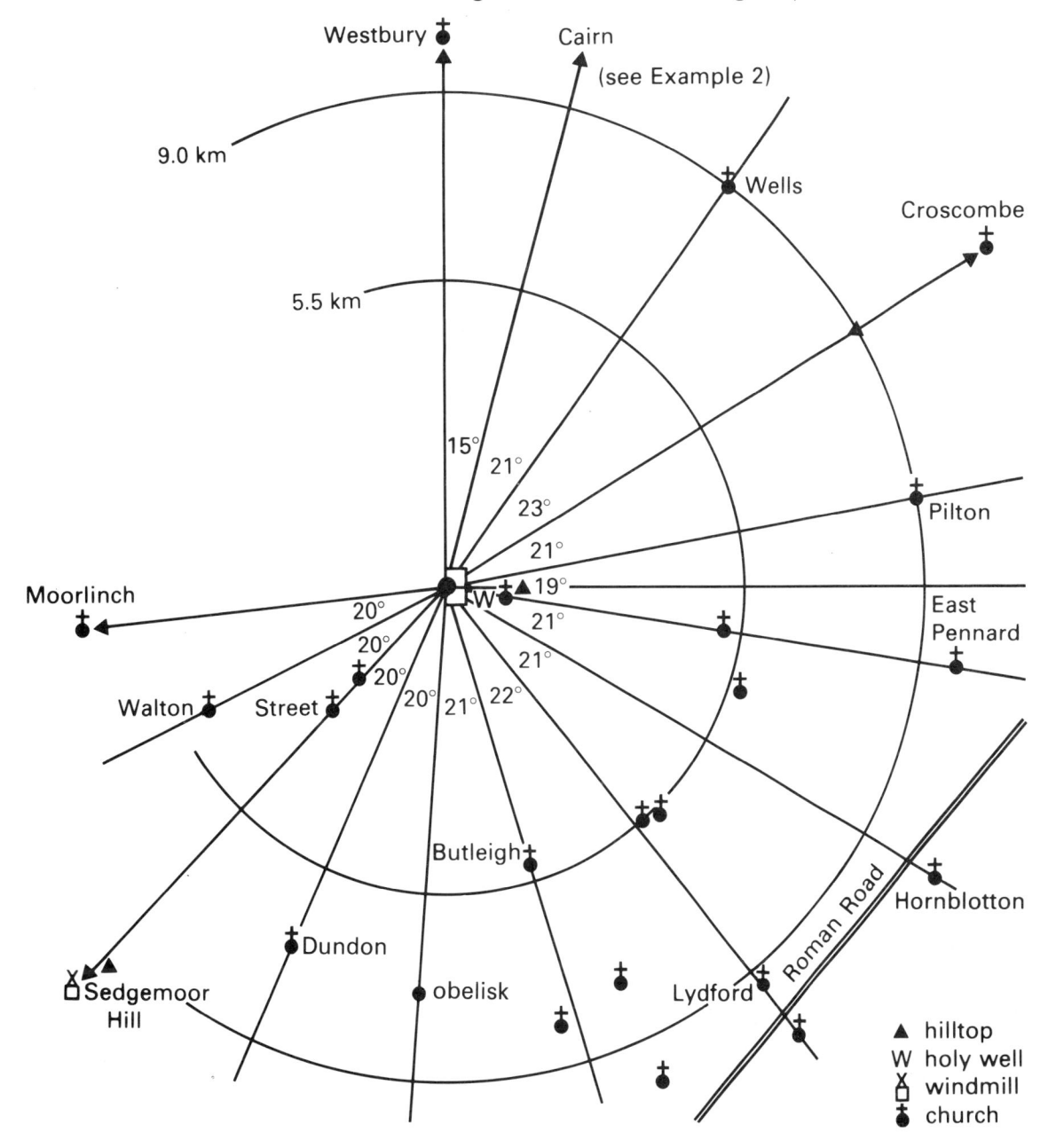

▲ PROJECT 2

One of the most mysterious features of the British landscape is the large number of stone circles, or **henges,** whose original purposes and methods of construction have never been fully understood. Stonehenge and Avebury (Wiltshire), the Rollright Stones (Oxfordshire) and Castlerigg Circle (Cumbria) are perhaps the most famous.

Such circles are often found to lie on precise alignments with other ancient sites (tumuli, churches, etc. – see Project 1), and their geometry often seems remarkably precise. The megalithic people who built them apparently knew quite a lot of mathematics.

On the following pages, the position and geometry of Castlerigg Circle (near Keswick, Cumbria) are partly described. You are invited to trace these plans and investigate the construction of the circle in more detail. Alternatively you could investigate any other circles that interest you – there are hundreds throughout Britain. You will find them on Ordnance Survey maps, and more detailed information can be obtained from the National Trust.

A good introductory booklet with many photographs is *Prehistoric Stone Circles* by A. Burl (published by Shire Publications, Aylesbury).

CASTLERIGG CIRCLE (OS REF. 292237): PLAN VIEW

The shape of the circle is a symmetrical ovoid, aligned north–south. Its dimensions are N–S 40 MY, E–W 35 MY; the inner trapezium has approximate dimensions 8 MY × 4 MY. There are 48 stones standing, numbered anticlockwise as shown below.

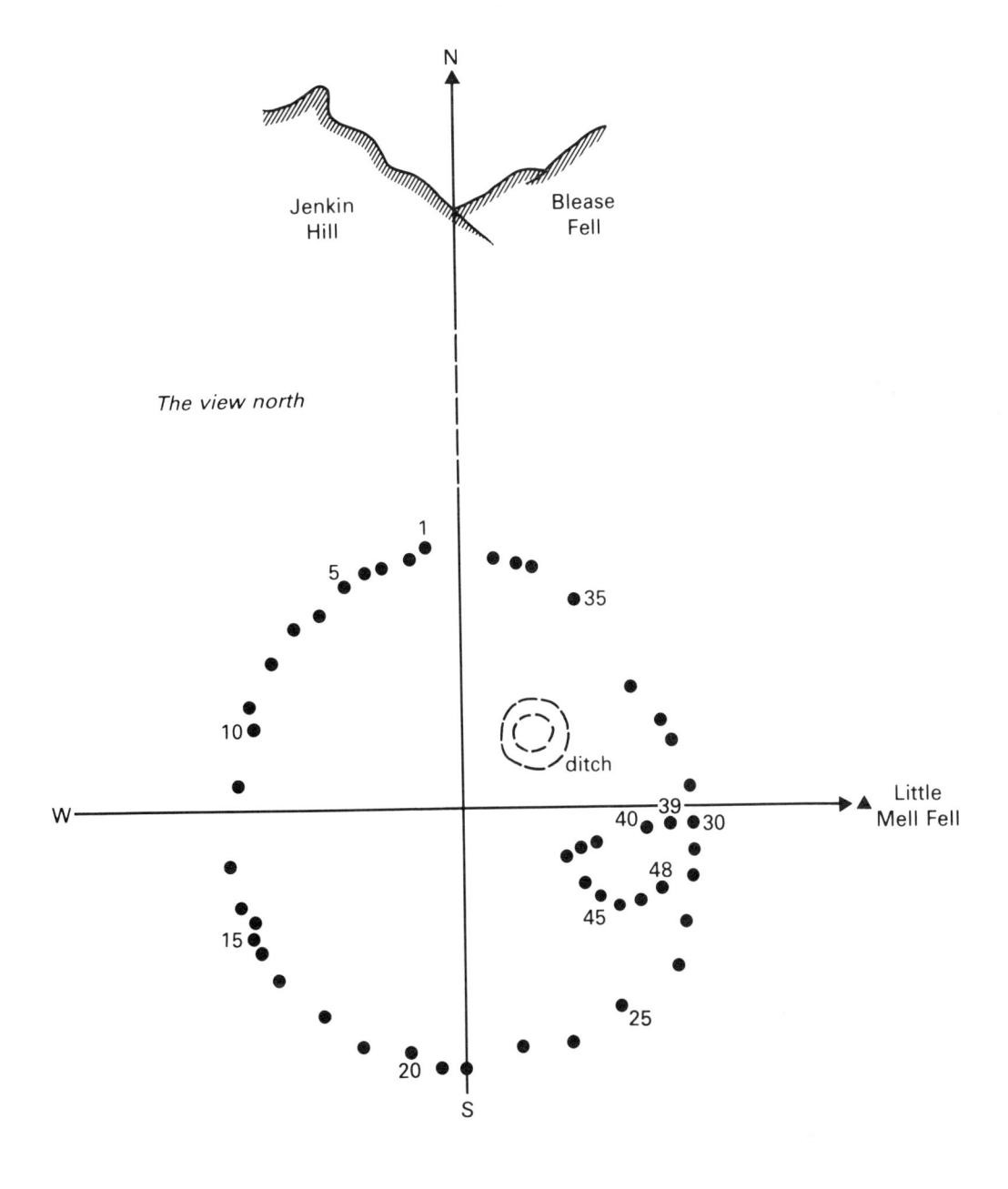

CASTLERIGG CIRCLE: GEOGRAPHIC POSITION

(Not to scale)

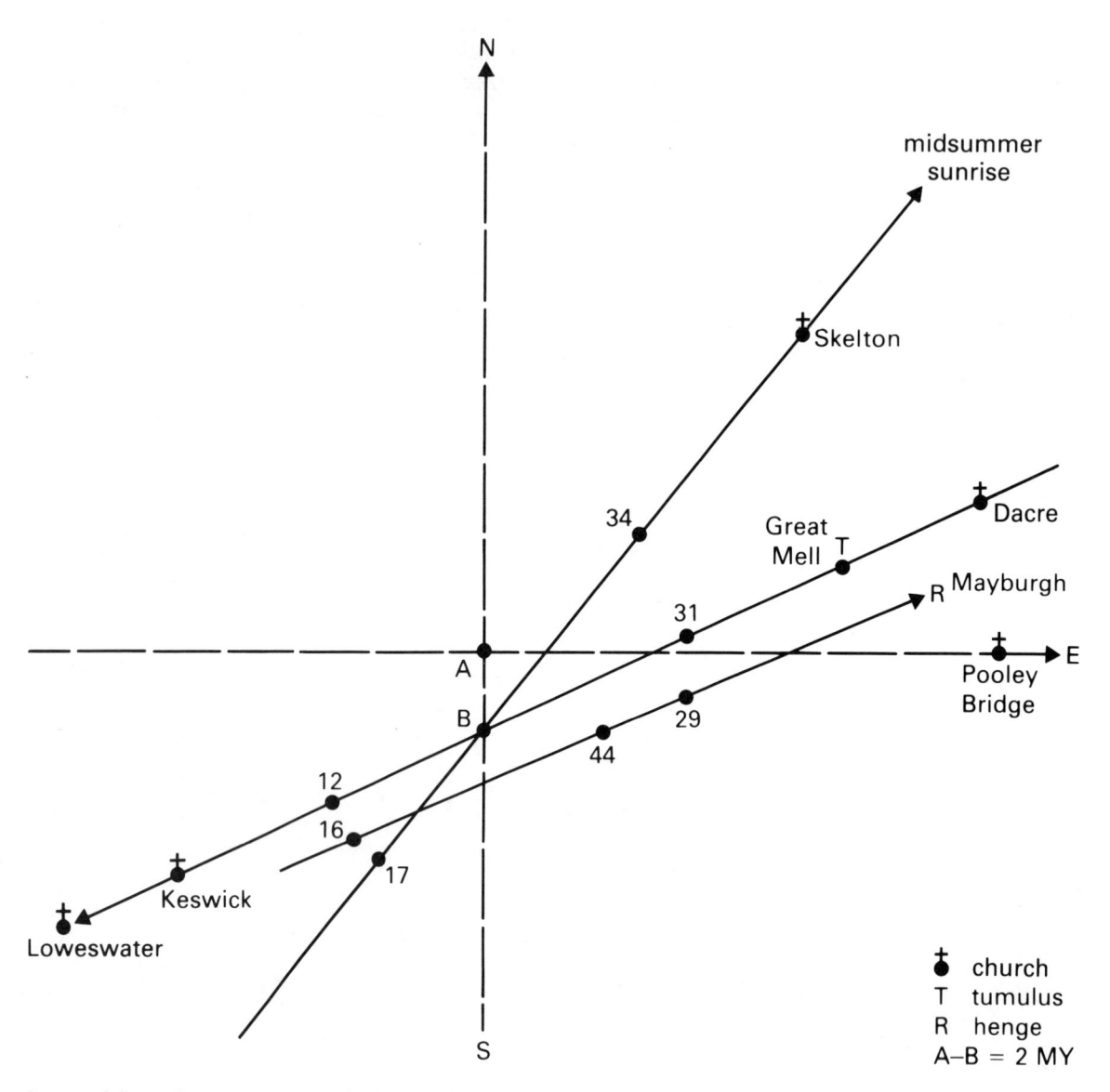

church — ✝●
T   tumulus
R   henge
A–B = 2 MY

Some hints for a geometric investigation
(i) Castlerigg Circle is actually egg-shaped, or ovoid. How would you construct such a shape? What is the simplest way of constructing it, without modern instruments?
(ii) If you use simpler goemetric shapes to 'build up' the ring (e.g. circles, triangles, etc.), measure their dimensions carefully in MY on your tracing of the

plan. To do this, measure the plan first and decide what scale has been used.

Note the simplicity of the dimensions given so far.

(iii) You should find that point B on the last diagram has a special geometric significance.

(iv) Some of the original stones are missing, and several others have obviously moved slightly from their original positions. However, most of them will not have moved much, if at all.

Try joining up the positions of the stones to each other and see if any regular geometric shapes are revealed. See whether lines joining stones on opposite sides of the ring intersect at interesting points.

Further work

It is difficult to believe that 'primitive' people could do accurate geometry (Castlerigg was built about 1500 BC). Try to imagine that you lived in those days with only the simplest of tools. How might you construct

(a) a straight vertical line
(b) a straight horizontal line
(c) a right angle ($\frac{1}{4}$ of a revolution)
(d) a circle
(e) parallel lines
(f) other important angles such as 30°, 45°, 60°, etc?

(See also Investigation 12 in Book 1.)

PROJECT 3

Surveyors use an instrument called a theodolite for measuring angles between lines joining up points on the landscape. In its simplest form it consists of a circular protractor (marked off with 0°–360°) on which a pointer revolves. The pointer is lined up with one landmark (A) and its position on the scale is noted. Then the pointer is revolved so that it is lined up with a second landmark (C), and its reading on the scale is taken again.

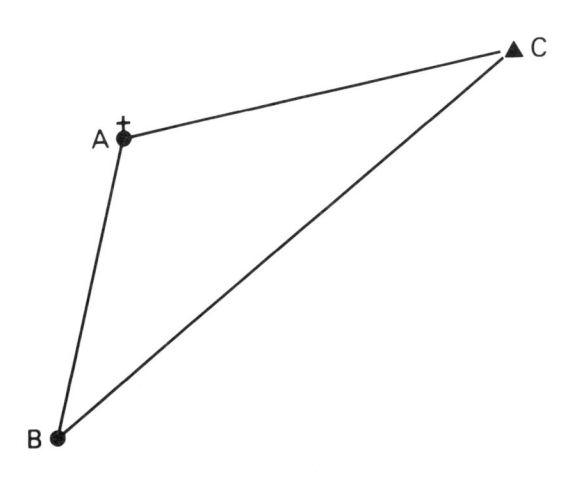

A surveyor at B aligns the pointer with the church at A; reading on the scale is, say, 43°.
The surveyor next aligns the pointer with the hilltop at C; reading now is, say, 75°.
Therefore, the angle $A\hat{B}C = 32°$.
The other angles could be found by the surveyor repeating the process, standing at A or C. If one or more of the distances between A, B and C are known, then the others can be calculated using the sine or cosine rules.
These methods are called **triangulation.**

The construction of a simple theodolite is described below. Working in a group, make an instrument and use it to measure angles and distances between points marked on your school playground or field. How could it be adapted to measure angles of elevation, and thus calculate heights of buildings?

SIMPLE THEODOLITE

Make a model in strong card first to become familiar with the principle, then use plywood or perspex.

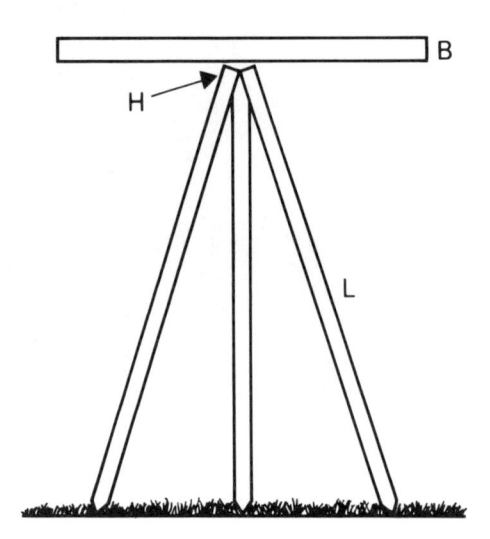

Side view

A solid base (B), say 40 cm square, supported by three legs (L) 1 m long, pointed at ground end and hinged to the base at H. Each leg can thus be moved independently in order to level the base.

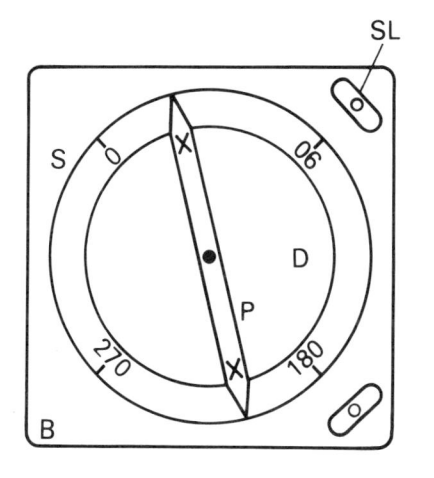

Plan view

The base (B) has two spirit levels (SL) to ensure it is horizontal. Fixed to the base is a scale (S), marked off in degrees, 36 cm diameter. A pointer (P) is fixed to a disc (D) of diameter 32 cm; the total length of the pointer is 36 cm. The disc is pinned at the centre of the board so that it is free to rotate.

For greater accuracy, sights may be mounted on the pointer at X. These could be ordinary rifle sights as shown below.

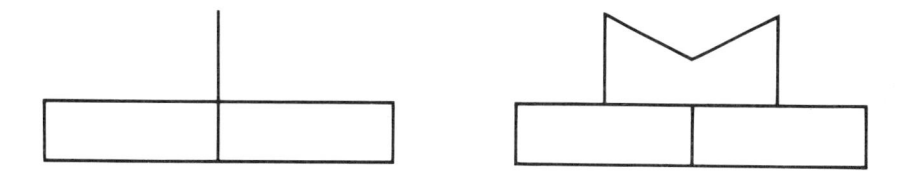

Alternatively, use a length of tube, 1 cm diameter, or a small telescope!

Measuring the world   10

▲ **PROJECT 1**

The Great Pyramid of Giza, in Egypt, is over four thousand years old and is known as one of the Seven Wonders of the World. It is not just remarkable for its size, or the fact that nobody is quite sure how (or why!) it was built. What is remarkable, as its structure is investigated in more detail, is the mathematical precision and significance of the design. The people of that time clearly knew much more mathematics than we sometimes give them credit for: they certainly knew about pi, about the golden ratio, and all about right-angled triangles – long before Pythagoras was born! In this project you will investigate some of the geometry and trigonometry of the Great Pyramid. Perhaps you will feel encouraged to go further, and investigate some of the theories about why it was built.

First, some reminders about π and ϕ.

(i) π is the ratio of the circumference of a circle to its diameter, and its value is 3.141 59, to five decimal places.
It is an irrational number which can never be written down precisely.
However, Egyptians did not use decimals but vulgar fractions (ratios); the simplest such approximation for π is 22 : 7. (See also Investigation 25 in Book 1.)

(ii) ϕ is the **golden ratio** found in the proportions of many living things (see Investigations 4 and 18 in Book 1).
It is an irrational number.
Its value is $(1 + \sqrt{5}) \div 2$, or 1.618 03 to five decimal places.
A vulgar fraction approximation is given by ratios

of successive terms of the Fibonacci sequence: 1, 1, 2, 3, 5, 8, 13, 21, 34,....

Thus 8 : 5 = 1.600 00, 13 : 8 = 1.625 00, 21 : 13 = 1.615 38, and so on. The higher the numbers used, the more accurate is the ratio to the value of φ.

There are several ways of evaluating φ by geometry, and you might like to investigate the following two.

1 The golden ratio is defined by dividing a line in such a way that the ratio of the whole line to the longer part equals the ratio of the longer part to the smaller part.

So $\dfrac{AC}{AB} = \dfrac{AB}{BC}$ or $\dfrac{1 + x}{x} = \dfrac{x}{1}$

Simplify and solve this equation.

2 Construct a rectangle of two equal squares.

Divide one square in half and draw the diagonal of the small rectangle formed.

Construct an arc on this diagonal as shown so that FH = FC.

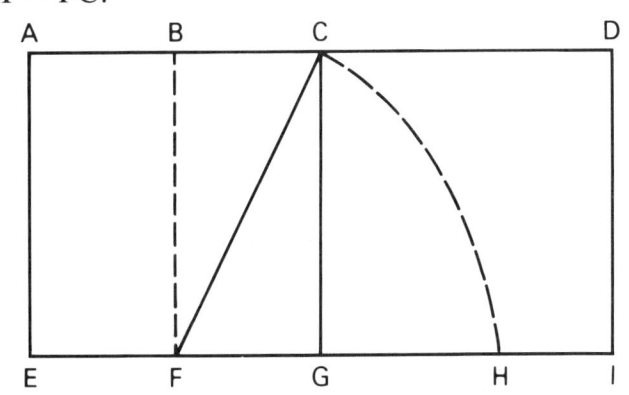

If AE = x then CG = x and FG = $x/2$. Use the *Theorem of Pythagoras* to calculate FC. (For simplicity you could let AE = 1 unit.)

Now, FH = FC and EF = $x/2$. So what is the length EH?

All of this brings us neatly back to the Great Pyramid, because the floor of the King's Chamber (the largest open space inside the pyramid) is indeed a rectangle constructed from two equal squares.

The design is a right pyramid with a square base. The special feature of this pyramid, however, is that the perimeter of the base equals the circumference of a circle whose radius is the height of the pyramid.
So if the height is h, the perimeter of the base is $2\pi h$, and the length of one side is $\pi h/2$.

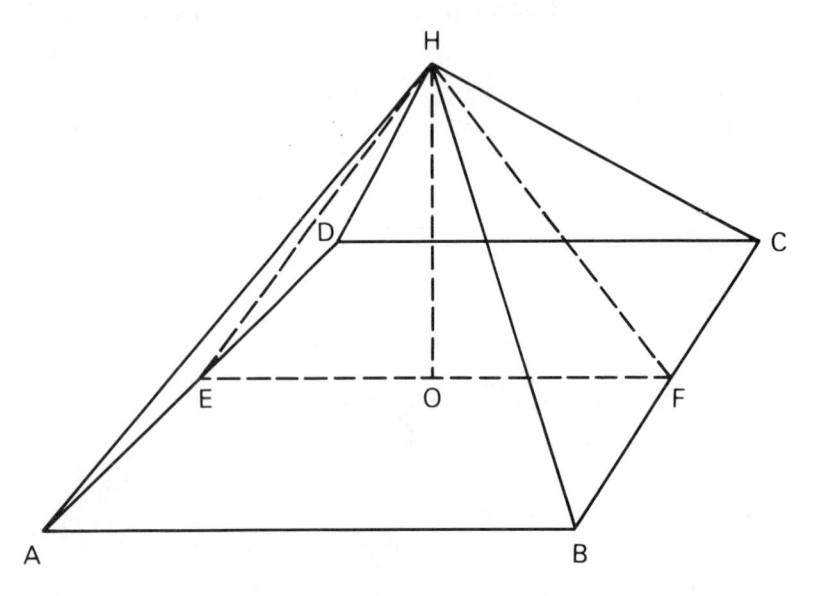

One further interesting fact is that the pyramid is aligned almost exactly true north–south–east–west. Make a copy of the diagram of the pyramid, and sketch neatly the following triangles

ABD, BOH, HEF, HOF, BHC and BHF.

What sort of triangles are they?
You should now use these triangles, and basic trigonometry, to find all the lengths and angles of the pyramid. The unit of measurement to use is the *royal cubit*. (1 royal cubit = 0.415 m = 16.3 inches or exactly half of one megalithic yard — see Investigation 9.)
The height of the pyramid is 280 cubits (OH).
Calculate
(a) the length of the base (BC)
(b) the height of one face (HF)
(c) the length of the edge (HB)
(d) the area of one face (HBC)
(e) the area of the cross section (HEF)
(f) the angle of slope of the face (HFO)
(g) the angle of slope of the edge (HBO)

(h) the base angle of the face (HBF) – if you know about circular measure, find this angle in radians too.

Calculate the ratios
(i) height of face to half of base (HF : OF)
(j) area of face to square of height (HBC : OH²)
(k) square of height to area of cross section, all squared ((OH² : HEF)²).

Taking your result for HF : OF as φ, calculate
(l) $4 \div \sqrt{\phi}$
(m) $\phi^2 \times 6/5$

If you have carried out these calculations carefully you should have discovered some very surprising results.

Further investigations
(n) Find the ratios of the lengths of the sides in triangle HOB – are any of them significant?

(o) What difference does it make to the calculations if π is taken as its value on a calculator, or as the ratio 22 : 7?

(p) The last question leads us to wonder just which ratios the ancient Egyptians actually used for π and φ.

Let us study the relationship you used in calculation **(l)** above. It is derived as follows.

IF OH = h, then OF = $\dfrac{\pi h}{4}$

By Pythagoras

$$HF^2 = h^2 + \left(\dfrac{\pi h}{4}\right)^2 = h^2\left(1 + \dfrac{\pi^2}{16}\right)$$

So $(HF : OF)^2 = 1 + \dfrac{16}{\pi^2} = \phi^2$

But $\phi^2 = \phi + 1$ (see your equation in **(l)** above)

So $\phi = \dfrac{16}{\pi^2}$ or $\pi = \dfrac{4}{\sqrt{\phi}}$

Using these relationships
(i) find φ, if π has its calculator value
(ii) find φ, if π is 22/7
(iii) find π, if φ is 13/8 (Fibonacci terms)

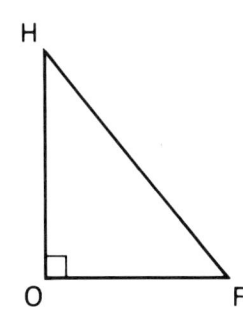

- (iv) find π, if ϕ is 21/13 (Fibonacci terms)
- (v) find π, if ϕ is 34/21 (Fibonacci terms)
- (vi) continue to use ratios of higher Fibonacci terms to calculate π and decide which ratio the Egyptians might have used.

(q) The other relationship between π and ϕ, used in calculation (m) above, comes from a diagram of a human figure found in the tomb of the pharaoh Rameses 9th, which again proves the Egyptians had advanced knowledge of trigonometry.

The sides LM and MN of the right-angled triangle are formed by a snake, and measure 3 units and 4 units respectively.

Thus the pharaoh's height is 5 units. The length c is 1 unit.

The ratio, length of leg: remaining body as shown, that is, $a : b$, equals $\phi : 1$, so the height of the body is represented by parts $\phi + 1$, or ϕ^2.

If this is 5 units, and NP is 1 unit, then the length LP is $\phi^2 \times 6/5$. This equals π correct to four decimal places! Investigate the accuracy of this relationship using the approximations for π and ϕ given earlier.

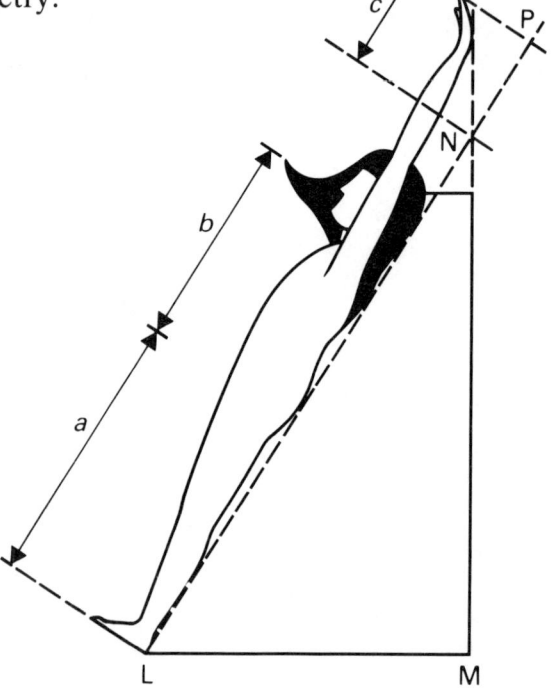

(r) Of the many theories as to why the Great Pyramid was built, two in particular catch the imagination. One is that it had mystical or religious purposes and that its design caused it to concentrate spiritual energy. Some experiments in recent years have suggested there might actually be something in this. For example, it is said that if a perfect scale model is constructed and aligned north-south, organic matter (such as fruit) placed inside will be preserved, or blunt razor blades will become sharp. It is also said that the effect is greater if the object is placed one third of the way up the central axis – can you think why?

You could test these ideas by making scale models of the Great Pyramid; you could also try using different geometric models (cone, cuboid, etc.) as a 'control'. Does the material used to make the model affect the result? Does it matter if you use an open frame model?

■ PROJECT 2

The second theory of the pyramid's purpose is rather harder to grasp, but especially fascinating.
It is said that the pyramid's surface was an accurate map of the Northern Hemisphere, the apex being the North Pole, the base representing the equator, and each face representing one quadrant of the hemisphere. For any map to be accurate, the curved surface of the Earth must be represented on a flat surface in perfect proportion; this is, as you might expect, particularly difficult.

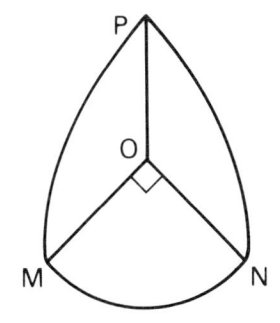

In the diagram, P is the North Pole, O is the centre of the Earth, M and N are points on the equator 90° apart.

So the diagram represents one quarter of the Northern Hemisphere.
The surface area of a sphere of radius R is $4\pi R^2$ and its circumference is $2\pi R$ (along an 'equator').
So for the quadrant shown
● the curved surface area is $\frac{1}{2}\pi R^2$
● the length of the arc MN is $\frac{1}{2}\pi R$.
Now, to make the comparison with the pyramid easier to see, suppose that the radius of the Earth is represented by a length equal to $\sqrt{\phi}$, and remember that $\pi = 4 \div \sqrt{\phi}$.
The surface area of one quadrant of such a model would be

$$\frac{1}{2} \times \frac{4}{\sqrt{\phi}} \times (\sqrt{\phi})^2 \quad \text{or} \quad 2 \times \sqrt{\phi}$$

and the length of arc along the equator would be

$$\frac{1}{2} \times \frac{4}{\sqrt{\phi}} \times \sqrt{\phi} \quad \text{or} \quad 2 \text{ units.}$$

So the curved surface of the quadrant could be represented accurately by a triangle with base 2 units (representing ¼ of the equator) and area $2\sqrt{\phi}$ *or* any multiple of this.

But the cross section triangle of the Great Pyramid *is* just such a triangle (HEF in the earlier diagram).

If the base $\frac{1}{2}\pi h = 2$ units,
then $h = 4/\pi = \sqrt{\phi}$ units.
The area of HEF = $\sqrt{\phi}$ units.

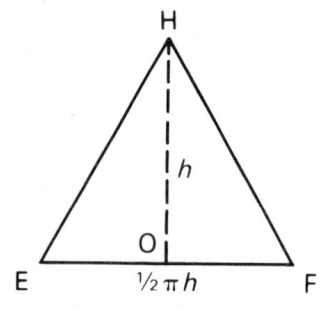

This triangle is therefore a scale representation of one quadrant of the Northern Hemisphere. You may object that each quadrant is supposed to be represented by a triangular *face* of the pyramid, and this triangle (HBC) has a different area to the cross section (although its base is the same).

However, imagine that you are standing looking at the pyramid from a little distance.

Perhaps you would like to investigate this or other methods of map projection further. For more information about all these projects, a good book to use is *Secrets Of The Great Pyramid* by P. Tompkins (published by Penguin).

■ PROJECT 3

This project requires groupwork and considerable organisation, but it is very worthwhile. You are going to measure the Earth itself.

It is a method that has been used by many mathematicians since ancient times, and it can be very accurate.

The diagram below shows the Earth with the sun's rays falling on it (the sun is so far away, these rays may be assumed to be parallel). P and Q are two places on the *same* longitude. XP and YQ are vertical poles of equal height, which cast shadows PM and QN respectively. If the lengths of these shadows are measured on *horizontal* surfaces, then the triangles XPM and YQN are right-angled.

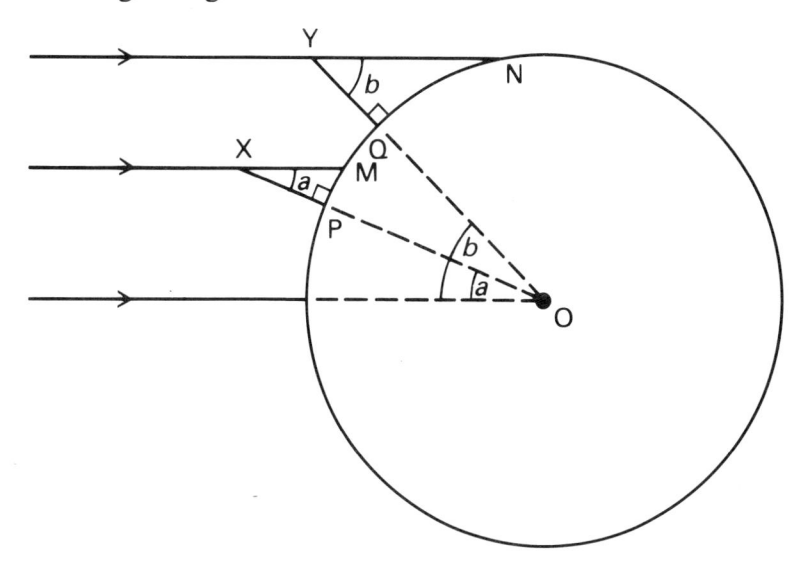

$$\text{Tan } a = \frac{PM}{XP} \quad \text{and} \quad \tan b = \frac{QN}{YQ}$$

Now consider the sector OPQ. The arc PQ is the same fraction of the circumference as the angle $b - a$ is of one revolution.

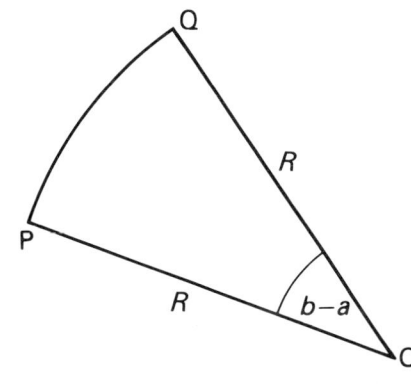

$$\frac{PQ}{2\pi R} = \frac{b - a}{360°}$$

$$\text{so} \quad R = \frac{180° \times PQ}{\pi \times (b-a)}$$

(If the angles are measured in radians this simplifies to $R = PQ/(b-a)$.)

Thus the radius of the Earth can be calculated if the distance between the two points P and Q is known, and the angles *a* and *b* are measured.

(a) Using a good quality map, find another town or city in Britain (or France or Spain!) which is on the same longitude as yours. Contact the Education Department there for names and addresses of schools that might be willing to cooperate with you.
(b) When you are in touch with a group in another school, agree details such as the length of the pole to be used, how to measure its shadow and, above all, the exact date and time of the experiment. Remember to choose alternatives in case the day you choose isn't sunny!
(c) On the map, measure the distance between your schools in a direct line as accurately as possible.
(d) After the experiment, exchange information about the angles you have measured.

PROJECT 4

This work could form an interesting extension of the earlier projects on ley lines or the Great Pyramid. It involves some quite advanced ideas in arithmetic and trigonometry.

Studies of many ancient monuments especially in Egypt and Greece reveal that the people who constructed them had developed a detailed, accurate and very rational system of measures: length, volume, weight and time were all interrelated and all based on one fundamental unit of length. (Indeed, the system has been preserved in the British Imperial system of measures.)

(i) The basic unit was the **foot,** equivalent to 300 mm. For reasons too complicated to go into here, the Egyptians also defined the **geographic foot** = 307.8 mm.
(What is the metric equivalent of the British foot?)
1 foot = 4 hands or 16 fingers
$1\frac{1}{2}$ feet = 1 cubit
600 geographic feet = 1 stadium
1 cubit + 1 hand (= 7 hands) = 1 royal cubit
What are the British and metric equivalents of these units? You should find an interesting relationship between the royal cubit and the

British foot. (The **inch** was introduced later by the Romans; it was equivalent to the width of the thumb.)

(ii) The average speed of marching or rowing was assumed to be 30 stadia per hour, for a maximum of 10 hours a day. The average sailing speed was thought to be $1\frac{1}{4}$ × rowing speed, for up to 24 hours a day.
What are these speeds in British and metric units, and how far did Egyptians reckon to travel in a day?

(iii) Now, 600 stadia were reckoned equivalent to 1° of arc for Mediterranean and Middle-East sailors. How many feet and cubits is this? What is the relationship with *time*?

For each of these cases, using the values of the units given earlier, calculate the radius of the Earth and assess its accuracy.

(**Hint** Circumference = 360° of arc, $R = C/2\pi$.)

(a) The cubit (= $1\frac{1}{2}$ geographic feet) was reckoned as 1/1 800 000 of the length of Egypt, which occupied $7\frac{1}{2}°$ of arc (to Aswan in the south).

(b) At the equator, 1 stadium was reckoned to be equal to 351.6 royal cubits.

(c) In England, in about 930 AD, a distance called 'the King's girth' was defined as 18 250 imperial feet and was reckoned as equivalent to one twentieth of one degree of arc.

(iv) It was mentioned earlier that the royal cubit was 7/6 of a standard cubit, and there were special reasons for this. In particular, the number 7, the Egyptian national symbol, was regarded as sacred, and the 'link between Earth and the order of the heavens'. But even more than this, the number 7 is extremely useful in simplifying practical calculations.

(d) Agricultural units of area were defined in a sequence, each being double the last.
The basic unit was 70 cubits square. (Compare the

imperial acre = 70 square yards, or 10 square chains.)

The double of this was taken to be 100 cubits square.

The double of this was taken to be 140 cubits square.

The double of this was taken to be 200 cubits square, and so forth.

For greater accuracy, the diagonal of a square unit was taken as 10/7 or 14/10 of the side.

Investigate the accuracy of these estimates.

(e) To define angles of 30° and 60°, the height of an equilateral triangle is $\sqrt{3}/2$ of its side. This was in practice taken as the ratio 6 : 7.
How accurate is the estimate?

(f) π was taken to be 22/7 – how accurate is this?

(g) These examples show that 7 can be used to produce simple but good approximations for irrational numbers such as $\sqrt{2}$, $\sqrt{3}$ and π. The Egyptians also used the number 11 in a similar way.
Investigate how other important irrational numbers might be estimated using 7 and 11.

(h) To help potters, a simple formula was devised to enable a cylindrical vessel to be constructed equal in volume to a given cubic volume.
If the width and height of a given cuboid are both increased by a factor 11/10, these measures can be taken as the diameter and length of an equivalent cylinder.

EXAMPLE

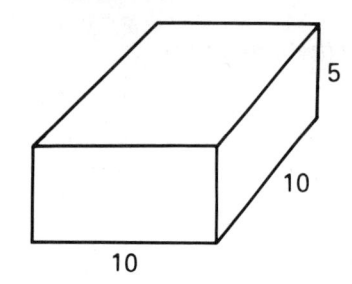

Width   10 cm
Height 5 cm
Volume 500 cm^3

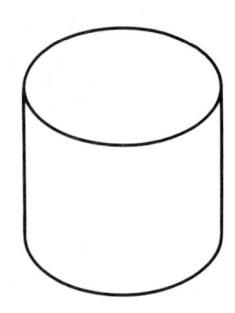

Diameter   11 cm
Length   5.5 cm
Volume ?

Investigate the accuracy of this method.
You should find that the cylinder's volume is actually slightly too great. But why would that be a good thing?

(i) If you have done Investigation 18 in Book 1, you may be interested in this project which takes the geometry of the pentagon further. In particular you will discover some fascinating angle relationships which the ancient Egyptians knew and used extensively.

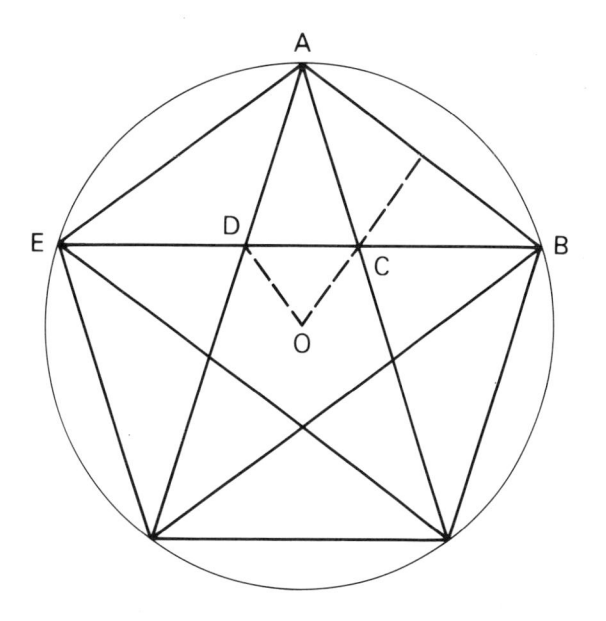

Angle DOC = 72° and of course the figure is symmetrical. Let the length DC = 1 unit, AD = x.
Identify all the angles in the figure.
Now, using triangle ADC, show that

(a) $\sin 36° = \dfrac{\sin 72°}{x}$ (*the sine rule*)

(b) $\cos 36° = \dfrac{2x^2 - 1}{2x^2}$ (*the cosine rule*)

(c) The *double angle rule,* which you have probably not met before, states that
$$\sin 2A = 2 \times \sin A \times \cos A$$

Hence $\sin 72° = 2 \times \dfrac{\sin 72°}{x} \times \dfrac{2x^2 - 1}{2x^2}$

Simplifying and solving this equation gives

$$x = \frac{(1 + \sqrt{5})}{2}, \text{ which equals } \phi.$$

Confirm also that $\phi^2 = \phi + 1$.
Use $x = \phi$ to evaluate the ratios ED : DC, EC : ED, EB : EC, and AB : AC.
It is not surprising that the pentagon and pentacle were regarded as magical by ancient people. But there are further surprises when the angles of the figure are investigated.

You have already shown, in (a), that $\dfrac{\sin 72°}{\sin 36°} = \phi$

Now use $x = \phi$ in the equation of (b) to find $\cos 36°$.
In the same triangle, use the *cosine rule* again to find $\cos 72°$.
Finally, using the *complementary angle rule* with these results, you can derive expressions for $\sin 54°$ and $\sin 18°$.

If you are mathematically ambitious, investigate how the *double angle rule* can be used with these simple results to evaluate the trigonometric ratios for other angles...!
Hint It will also be helpful to use the relationship $\sin^2 A + \cos^2 A = 1$

(j) Now, the angle 36° proves extremely significant apart from its occurrence in the pentagon and the fact that it is a simple 1/10 of a revolution. Consider the following triangle.

AC = 100 units
AB = 123.61 units
BC = 72.65 units
Angle BAC = 36°

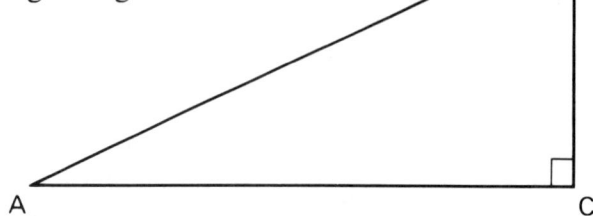

In construction work, this triangle was often approximated to

AC = 100
AB = 123
BC = 72

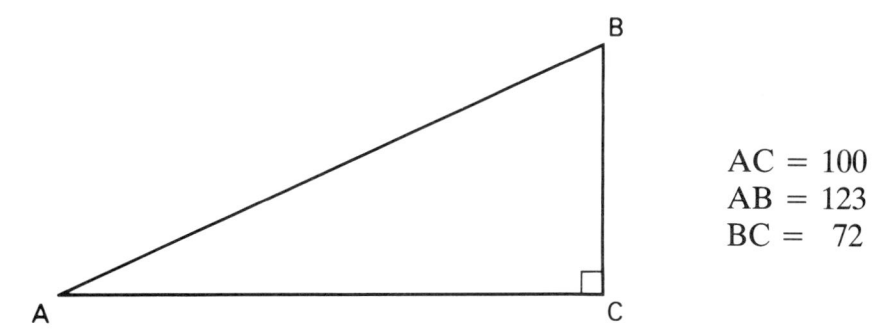

The length of 123 units is often found in ancient Egyptian architecture. What is the error in the sides and angles when making this approximation? The last triangle was considered important because it, in turn, is an approximation of

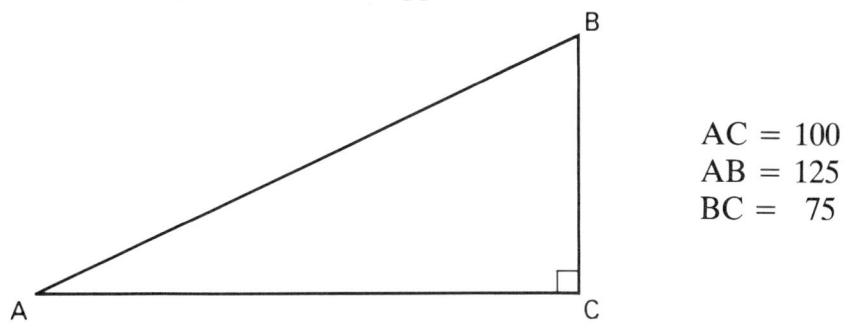

AC = 100
AB = 125
BC = 75

This last figure is of course a basic 3 : 4 : 5 'Pythagorean' triangle, which the Egyptians considered sacred.
What is the degree of error in making this approximation?
(You may be interested to know that the ratios 3 : 4 : 5 are the basic proportions of the second Pyramid of Giza.)

Finally, how did the Egyptians and other ancient people actually measure angles accurately?
(Some clues are given in Investigation 12 of Book 1.)

Consider the angle 36°. It may have been defined using the φ relationship discovered in the last project, but a simpler method could be to divide a length of rope into ten equal parts and then stretch the rope into a circle (see diagram overleaf). If the radius of the circle is decided in advance, its circumference can be calculated thus giving the length of rope to be used.

Rope divided into
ten equal parts...

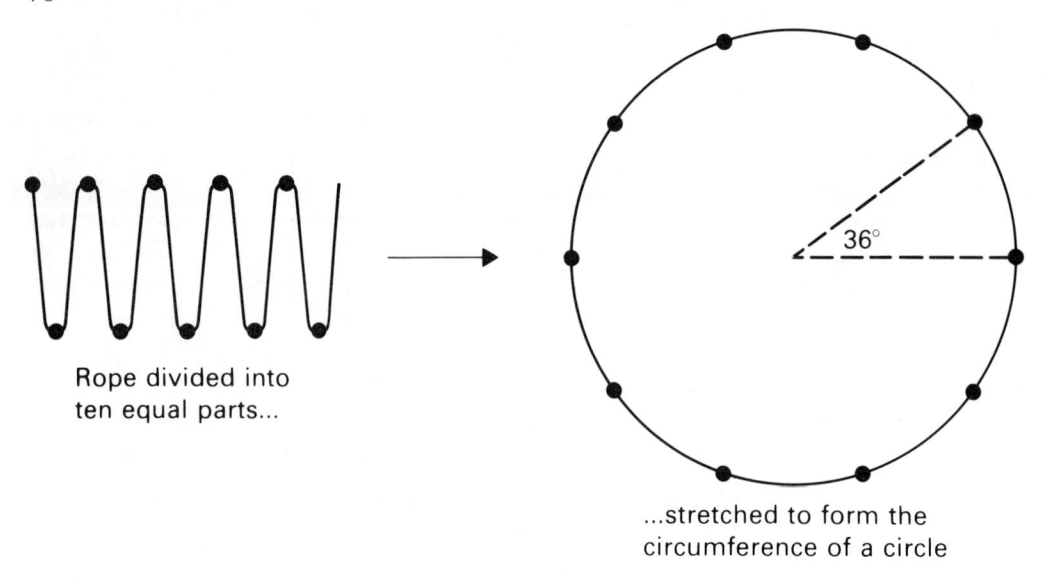

...stretched to form the
circumference of a circle

Many other angles could be defined in this way, as simple fractions of one revolution. But how much error would be involved in the calculation of angles if, in using this method, π was taken to be the approximation 22/7?

Measuring yourself   11

● **PROJECT 1**

On the next page is a copy of part of a famous ink drawing by Leonardo da Vinci, made in about 1492. It is called 'The Proportions Of The Human Figure'. Dotted line have been added at points da Vinci marked as significant.

Make careful measurements of the diagram and see what you can discover about human proportions.

EXAMPLES

Length of leg   = half full height
Height of knee = half length of leg

It is perhaps quite easy to see why da Vinci enclosed the figure in a square, but what is the significance of the circle? Find the ratio of the square's side to the circle's radius.

How well do *you* or members of your family conform to these proportions? Do the proportions depend upon a person's age?

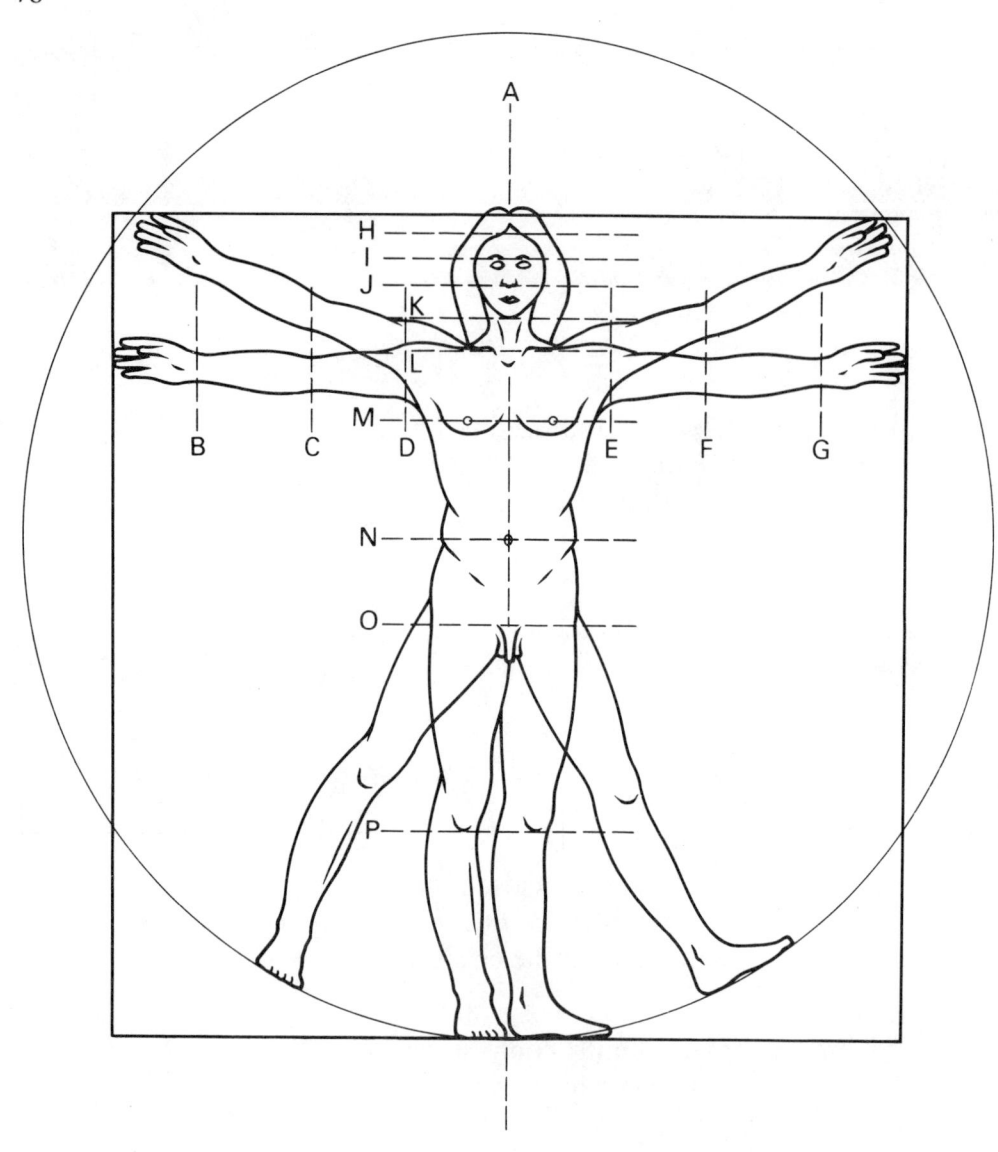

▲ PROJECT 2

On the next two pages are diagrams based on an extensive analysis of human skeletons by J. Hambidge. (First published by Yale University Press in *Diagonal*.)

Study the diagrams carefully and make accurate measurements. If you have done the last project, do the human proportions here agree with da Vinci's drawing? What are the important differences between male and female proportion?

How well do you or members of your family conform to these proportions?

Notice that the diagrams have been done especially to show the interrelationships between different points of the body. Several triangles and rectangles have thus been formed.
Measure angles, too, and comment on what you find. How many of the rectangles have ϕ proportions (length : width = approx. 1.62)?

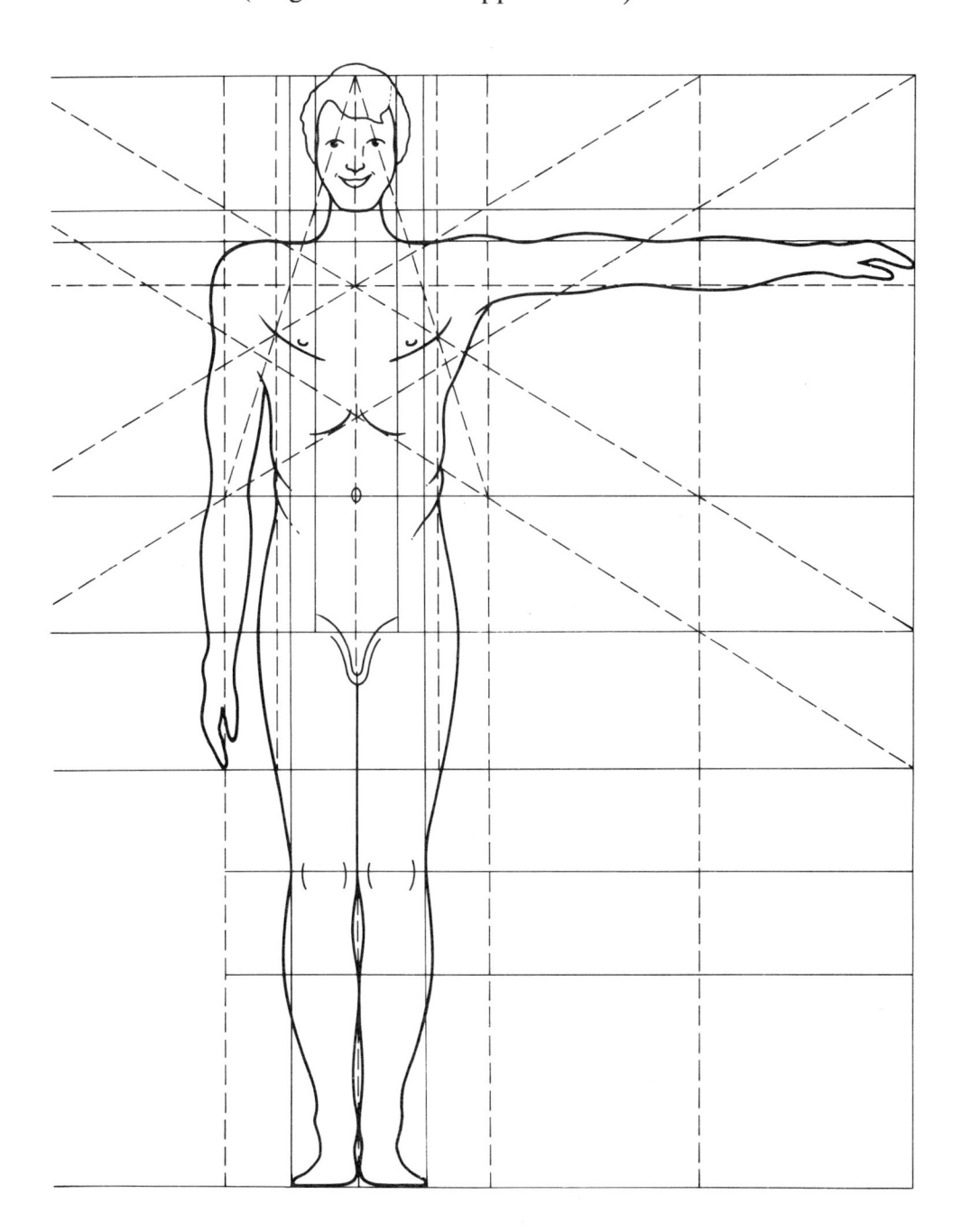

80

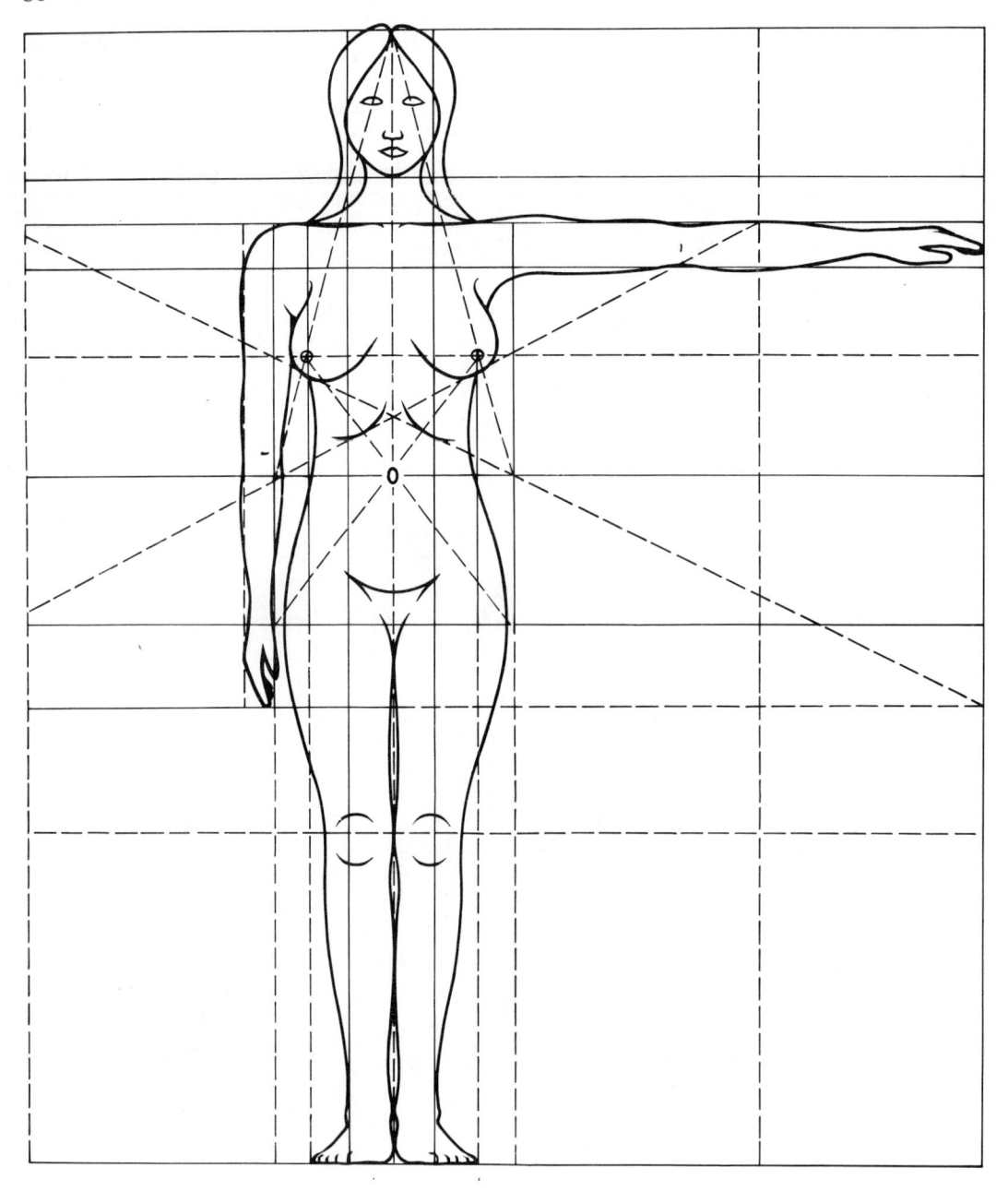

Loci and envelopes

12

● **PROJECT 1**

A **locus** is a path, or line, formed by a moving point. An **envelope** is a line formed by several other overlapping straight lines.

This project contains a range of loci and envelopes for you to draw and investigate, some familiar and others not so familiar.
For each one
- find out its name and describe its important characteristics;
- describe, with sketches, some of the practical uses these shapes are put to in the world and explain why they are suited to their purposes.

(a) Draw a large circle and mark off every 15° along the circumference to form 24 equally spaced points. Join each point to every other point.

(b) Imagine two pebbles dropped simultaneously into a pool of water a little distance apart. Their ripples form a very interesting pattern.
Draw two sets of equal, concentric circles so that they overlap each other. Mark the points where the smallest of one set crosses the largest of the other set, then the points where the next larger of the first set crosses the next smaller of the second set, and so on.

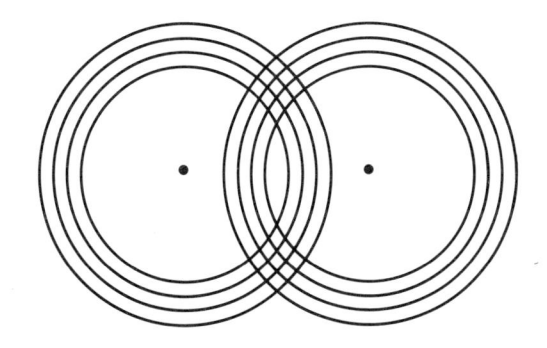

(c) Draw two long straight lines at an angle of about 30° and mark off equally spaced points on both. Label the points from left to right 1, 2, 3,... on each line.
Join the highest number on one line to the lowest number on the other with a straight line, then the next smaller on the first line to the next higher on the second line, and so on.

(d) Draw a set of axes and mark off −5 to +5 on each using a large scale. Join each point on the x-axis to its reciprocal on the y-axis (for example, $2 \to \frac{1}{2}$).

The four shapes you have created so far form a special group called **conic sections.** What do they have to do with cutting a cone?

(e) Draw a large circle and mark a point within it, away from the centre. Line up a set square so that one of its perpendicular edges touches the point and its right-angle touches the circumference of the circle. Draw chords along the two perpendicular edges of the set square.
Repeat this for many different positions of the set square.

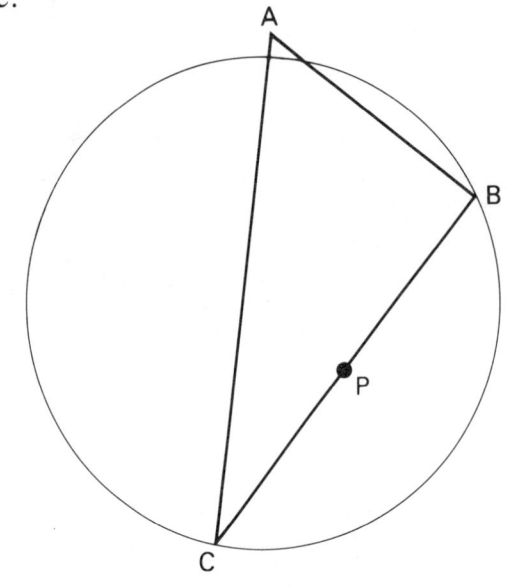

In the diagram, mark P in circle. Draw chords along AB, BC.

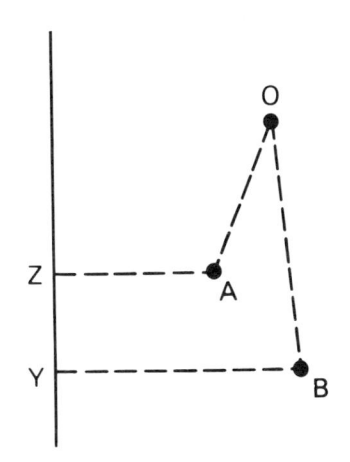

(f) Draw a straight line and a point, a little distance apart.
Now find several other points whose distance from the first point equals its perpendicular distance from the line.

$$OA = AZ$$
$$OB = BY$$

Find several more points like A and B.

(g) Mark two points A and B some distance apart on some paper. Cut a length of cotton about $1\frac{1}{2}$ times the length of the line AB. Fix the ends of the cotton at A and B with drawing pins.
Place a pencil against the cotton so that it is pulled taut. Move the pencil around on the paper, keeping the cotton taut all the time.

(h) Draw a set of axes and mark off -10 to $+10$ on each. Join (1,0) to (0,10), then (2,0) to (0,9), then (3,0) to (0,8), and so on.
Repeat this in each of the four quadrants.

(i) Draw a large circle and mark off every 10° to form 36 equally spaced points. Label them 1 to 36. Join up each number to its triple $(1 \rightarrow 3, 2 \rightarrow 6, 3 \rightarrow 9,$ and so on). When you reach a number greater than 36, subtract 36 from it (for example, $15 \rightarrow 45 - 36$ i.e. 9).

(j) What happens to the middle rung of a ladder when it slips down a wall?!

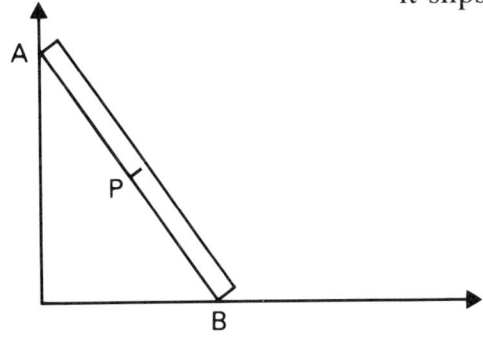

Draw a set of axes as shown and make a strip of card to represent the ladder; mark the middle point, P.
Now place the card as shown with the top, A, against the 'wall' and the base, B, on the 'ground'; mark the position of P. Move the 'ladder' up and down the wall to different positions, keeping

A and B on the axes, and mark P each time.
Extend the axes in the negative directions and
repeat the locus in all four quadrants.

(k) Repeat the last investigation but with P at a
different position on the card (a different 'rung' of
the ladder) – say, one third of the way up.
Try other positions for P.

(l) Repeat the last investigation but instead of marking
the position of P draw a line along the edge, AB, of
the card.

(m) What path does a point on the circumference of a
wheel follow as the wheel rolls along?
Draw a wheel in several positions as shown to
represent forward movement; the difference
between successive points of contact with the
ground should be one twelfth of the wheel's
circumference.

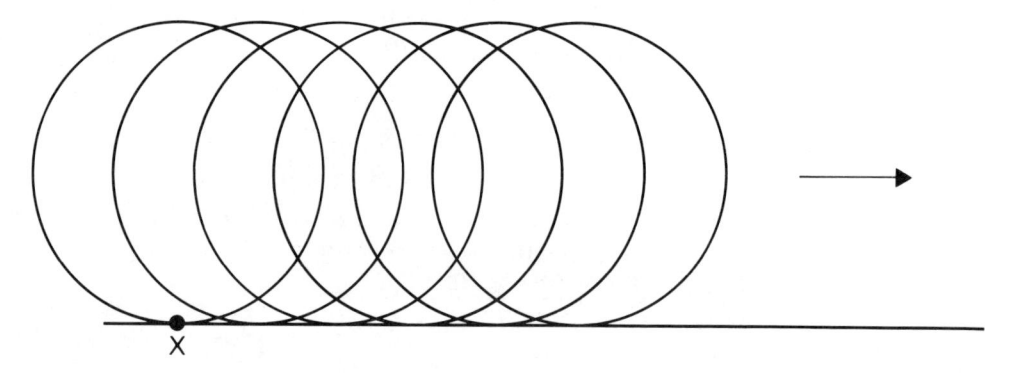

Now, consider point X at *6 o'clock* on the first
position of the wheel. If the wheel now moves
forward a distance 1/12 of its circumference, where
will X be on the second position?
Continue to plot its position as the wheel moves
forward.

Finally, here's an intriguing puzzle for you to
investigate and try to explain.

(n) Suppose a ball has a radius of 12 cm and a piece of
string is stretched around its 'equator'.

What is the length of the string?
Now suppose another piece of string exactly 1 m longer than the first could be stretched around the ball in a circle so that it is always a constant distance from the surface.
What would be the length of this string?
What would be the radius of the circle it describes?
How far from the ball's surface would it be?

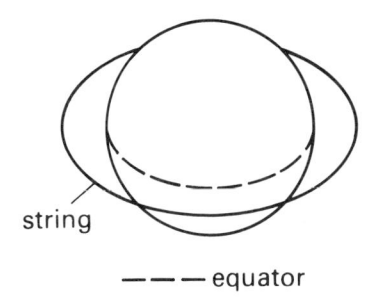

——— equator

In round figures, the radius of the Earth is 6400 km. If a piece of string is stretched round the equator, what is its length?
Now suppose another piece of string just 1 m longer than the first could be stretched round the Earth in a circle so that it is always a constant distance above the equator.
What would be the length of this string?
What would be the radius of the circle it describes?
How far from the Earth's surface would it be?

If your calculations are correct, your two final answers should be the same. But how can this possibly be true?

Reshaping

13

● **PROJECT 1**

The diagram below shows how a square may be cut into seven geometric shapes, called **tangrams**.
Study the diagram, then make your own set of tangrams with thick card.

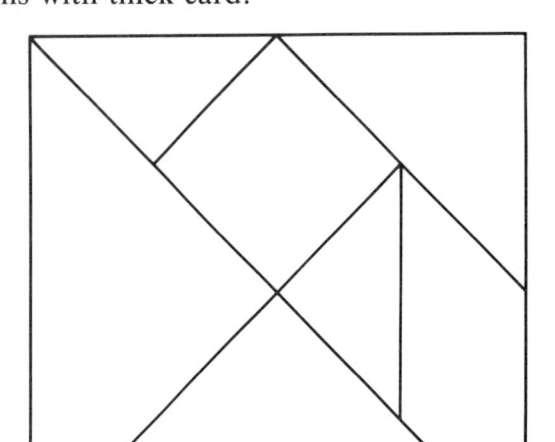

Investigate the angles and lengths of the sides of each shape, and their areas. Write a short summary of your findings, and describe the relationships between the shapes.

Now, these shapes can be reassembled in many different ways.
The diagram shows how all seven have been formed, without overlap, into a figure '1'.
Show how *all* the figures from '1' to '7' can be constructed using all seven tangrams for each, without overlap. It will be helpful if you use the relationships investigated earlier, for example, to decide which shapes can be put together to form straight lines.

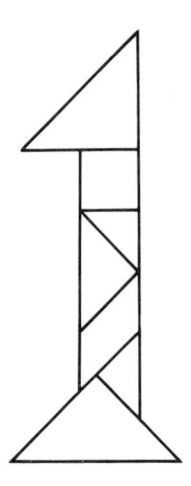

Can the seven tangrams be reassembled to form a rectangle?
Can they be formed into other geometric shapes? What other interesting figures can be formed?

If you would like to develop these ideas further, or as an alternative to this project, invent your own shapes by cutting a square or other figure in a different way and investigate how the pieces can be reassembled. An example is given below.

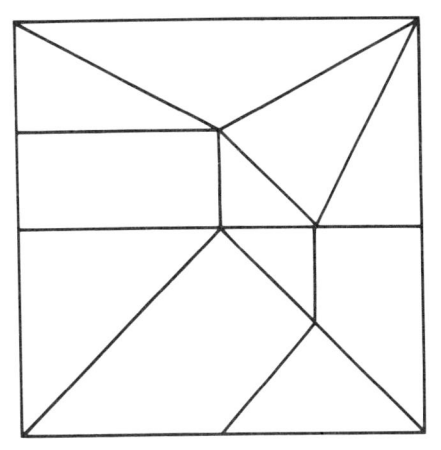

PROJECT 2

This project is in the form of paper-folding puzzles, so you will need a supply of squares of paper with a side of about 20 cm. However, you should also try to describe or prove your results using geometry and trigonometry. The first puzzle has been done in this way to show you the idea.

Puzzle 1
Fold a square into a regular octagon.

Method

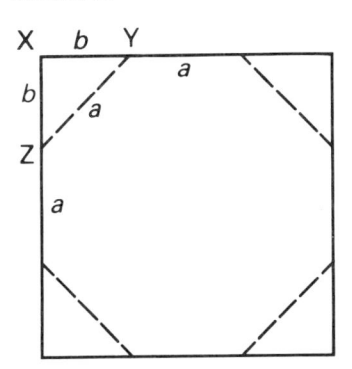

— — — folds

Description
Let each side of the octagon be a and the other lengths b.
Therefore side of square $= a + 2b$
In triangle XYZ
$$b^2 + b^2 = a^2 \quad \text{(Pythagoras)}$$
$$\therefore a = b\sqrt{2}$$

$\therefore$ side of square $= b\sqrt{2} + 2b$
$= b(\sqrt{2} + 2)$

So if side of square is 20 cm, the folds must be 20 ÷ (√2 + 2)
i.e. 5.86 cm from each corner.

Puzzle 2
Fold a square into a regular hexagon.

Puzzle 3
Fold a square to form an equilateral triangle (one method is shown).
What is the largest possible equilateral triangle that can be formed in a square?

Puzzle 4
Fold the bottom right-hand corner of a square (or rectangle) over to touch the left-hand edge.
How should this fold be made so that the crease AB is as short as possible?

Puzzle 5
What must the dimensions of a rectangle be so that it can be cut into five pieces, which can be reassembled to form a square?

Puzzle 6
Investigate other ways in which squares can be cut up so that the pieces may be reassembled into other geometric shapes.
(For example, see Project 1.)

Puzzle 7
What is the smallest rectangle from which the shape right could be formed, with the minimum number of pieces and the minimum waste? (All dimensions are to the nearest cm.)

Please send your solutions to the author, as this is a plan of his bathroom which is still uncarpeted!

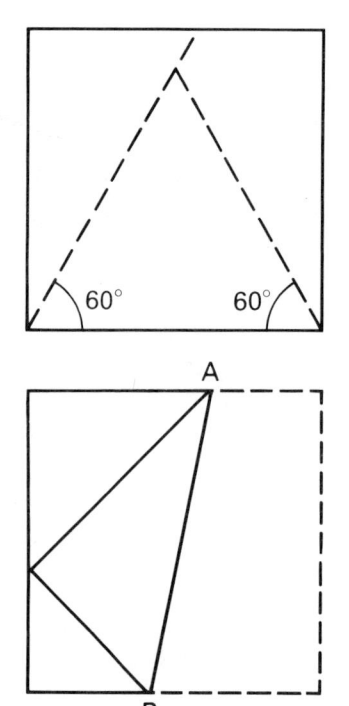

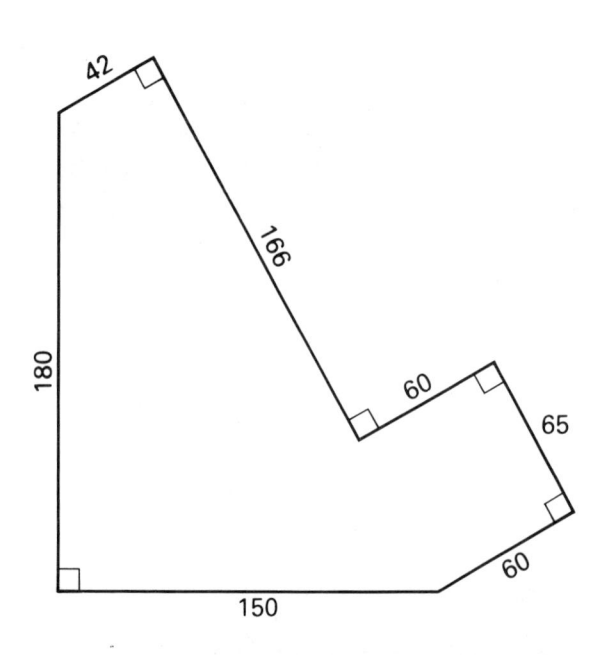

Relations

14

● **PROJECT 1**

Suppose that in *code f* each letter of the alphabet is replaced by the letter 7 places further along.
For example, A is replaced by H, N by U, Y by F.
The word HELLO would be written as OLSSV.

This operation could be described as $f : x \rightarrow x + 7$.
How could the *decoding* operation (called f^{-1}) be described?

Invent other similar codes and describe them, giving examples of their use. Explain also the decoding operation for each one.

▲ **PROJECT 2**

A code can be made even more effective by using two or more coding operations in succession.
For example, suppose code f is $f : x \rightarrow x + 7$ and code g is $g : x \rightarrow x - 2$. Then code gf can be defined as 'perform code f then perform code g on the result.'
Code gf is thus $gf : x \rightarrow (x + 7) - 2$, or $x \rightarrow x + 5$.
The word HELLO now becomes MJQQT.

Is code gf the same thing as code fg? Will your answer be true for any pair of codes of this sort?

How could the *decoding* of code gf, called $(gf)^{-1}$, be described? Would it be represented by $g^{-1}f^{-1}$ or by $f^{-1} g^{-1}$?

Investigate such multiple coding and decoding operations with two or three codes of your own.

● **PROJECT 3**

Below are some examples of logic flow-charts.
Study carefully how they are constructed, then try to make several of your own for other situations (for

example, crossing the road safely, playing badminton, making a cup of tea) and for similar puzzles.

1 Playing table-tennis (simplified)

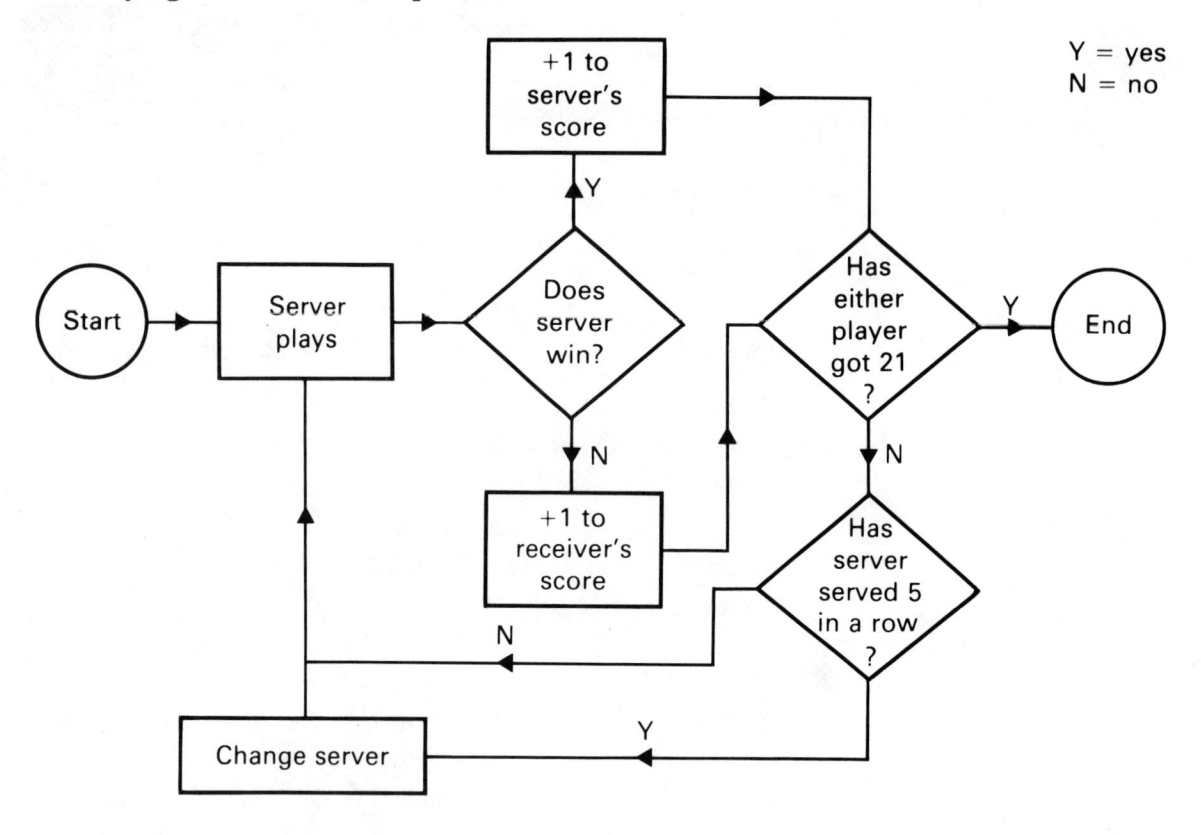

Y = yes
N = no

2 A puzzle
Think of a number; double it; add 8; double it; subtract 12; divide by 4; subtract the number you first thought of. The answer is 1!

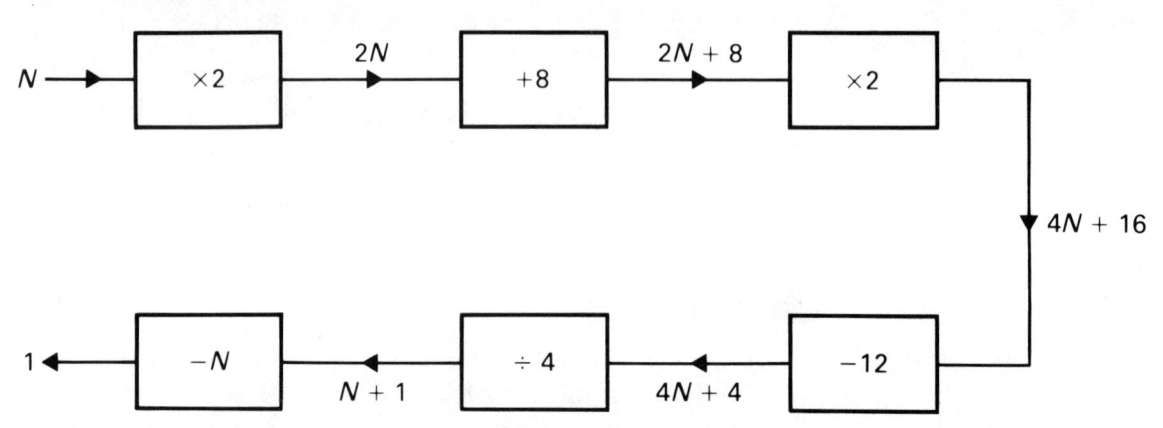

3 A plan for a computer program
What is its purpose?

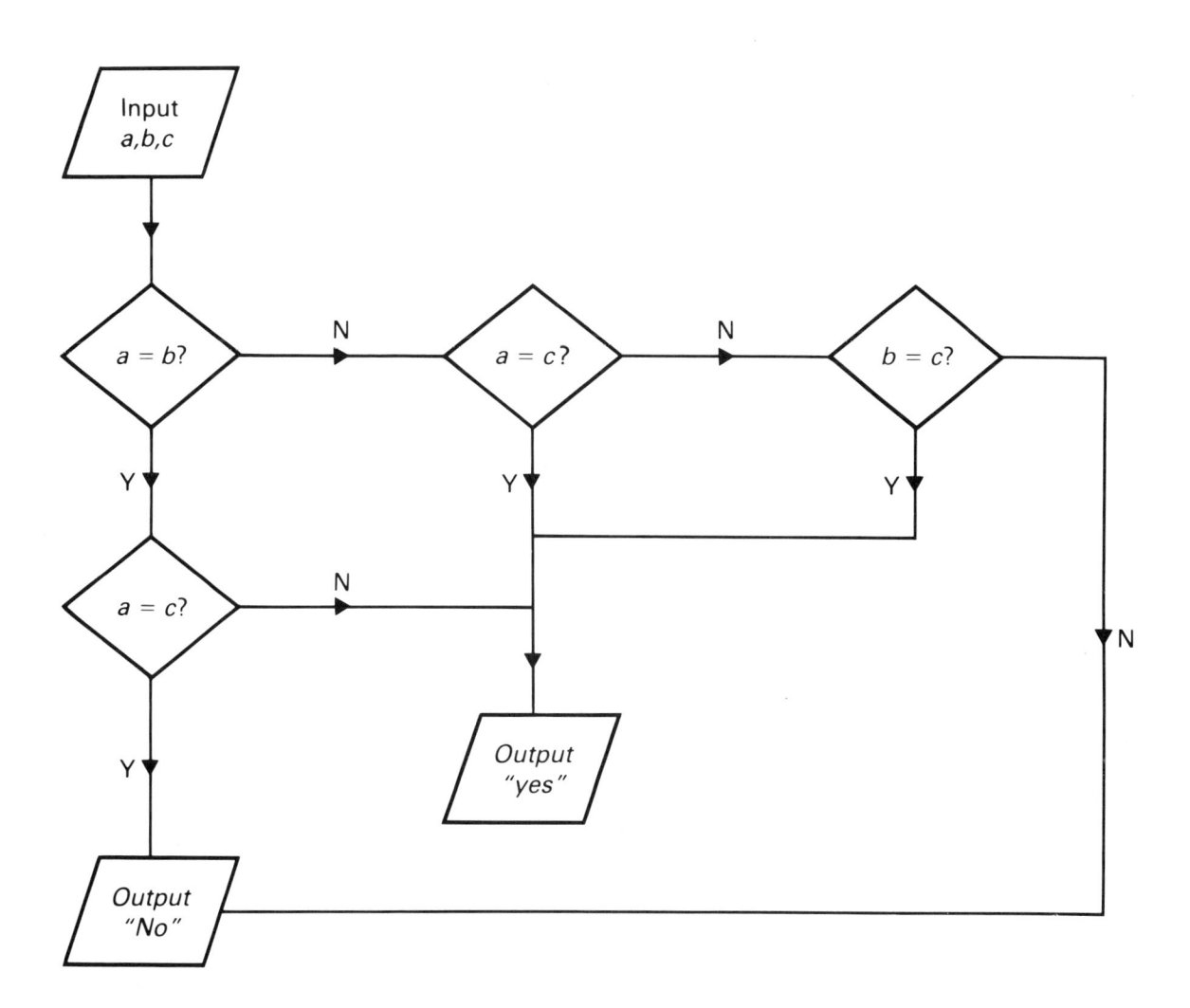

Write flow-charts for similar problems. (For example, given any three lengths, can they form a triangle and if so what kind? Given any five numbers, rearrange them in order or size, then find their mode, median and mean.)
Remember that the answer to a question in a flow-chart can only be 'yes' or 'no'.

PROJECT 4

A **nomogram** is a method of calculating which was popular before electronic calculators became widely available. It is still useful for demonstrating mathematical relations.

The chart below shows a relation between two sets of numbers, x and $f(x)$. Make a large-scale, accurate copy of it.

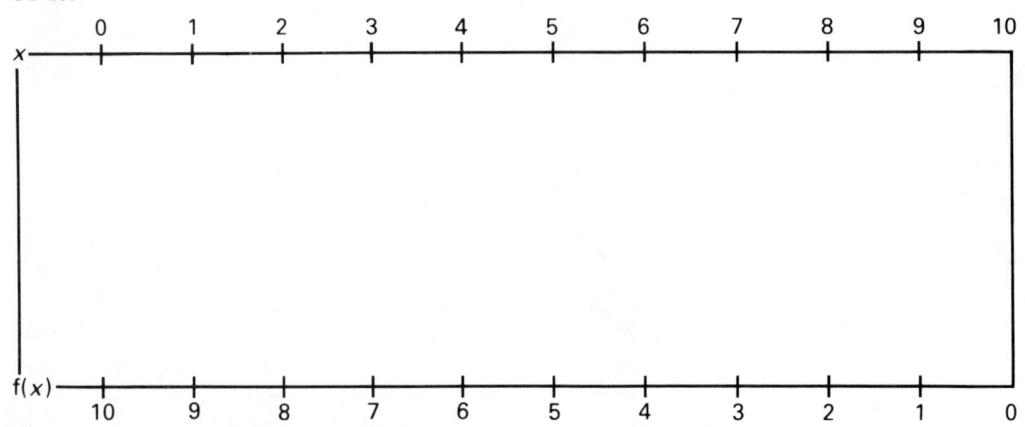

Now, using faint pencil lines
(a) join each number in x to the same number in $f(x)$, i.e. $f : x \to x$. What do you find?
(b) join each number in x to its double in $f(x)$ i.e.
   $f: x \to 2x$. What do you find?
Repeat this operation for
(c) $f: x \to 3x$ (d) $f: x \to 4x$ (e) $f: x \to \tfrac{1}{2}x$
and so on, until you have located several points. What is significant about these points?
Draw in the line $0 \to 0$ and call this line k.
Investigate the distances between points you have located along the k-line. Can you predict where other significant points would lie on this line?

The nomogram drawn expresses the relation

$$f(x) = kx \quad \text{or} \quad k = \frac{f(x)}{x}$$

Investigate how this nomogram can be used for
1 converting vulgar fractions into decimals;
2 doing simple decimal multiplications and divisions;
3 converting imperial/metric units (e.g. miles/km) or foreign currencies (e.g. £/$).

PROJECT 5

Individual nomograms (see Project 4) can be constructed for doing calculations with formulae that are used often.

EXAMPLE
Compare the formula
$$T = \frac{p-3}{2n}$$
with the original
$$k = \frac{f(x)}{x}$$

(i) $T \equiv k$, so relabel the k-line with T.
(ii) $p - 3 \equiv f(x)$ or $p \equiv f(x) + 3$. So replace each $f(x)$ number with $f(x) + 3$ and relabel this line p.
(iii) $2n \equiv x$ or $n \equiv x/2$. So replace each x number with $x/2$ and relabel this line n.

Now p can be calculated for given values of n and T. Alternatively, n can be found for given values of p and T.

Investigate the use of nomograms with formulae such as
$C = 2\pi r$; $A = \pi r^2$; $V = \frac{1}{3}\pi r^2 h$, and others.

Multiple upon multiple

15

● **PROJECT 1**

This project consists of several short investigations with numbers. At this stage, you are not expected to explain the results.

(a) Draw a grid as shown and continue it to at least 100.

1	2	3	4	5	6	7	8	9	10
11	12	13	14	15	16	17	18	19	20
21	22	23	etc.						

Strike out number 1.
Leave number 2, but strike out every second number after it (4, 6, 8, etc.).
Leave number 3, but strike out every third number after it (6, 9, 12, etc.).
Continue in this way, leaving the next available number in the grid but striking out every multiple of it that comes afterwards.

When you have finished, study the numbers that have not been struck out – what do they have in common?
Are there less or more of them as the numbers get bigger? (Count how many there are in each row.)
This method is attributed to a Greek mathematician called Eratosthenes.

(b) Draw another grid as before but with a different number of columns (the example below shows six). Now identify any square within your grid, made up of at least four positions.
Multiply the top left corner number by the bottom right corner number. Multiply the top right corner number by the bottom left corner number.
Find the difference between the two products.

1	2	3	4	5	6
7	8	9	10	11	12
13	14	15	16	17	18
19	20	21	22	23	24
25	26	27	28	29	30
31	32	33	34	35	36

In the square marked:
1st product = 14 × 28
= 392
2nd product = 16 × 26
= 416
Difference = 24

Repeat this for several squares of different sizes within your grid.
What is the relationship between your answer each time and the number of columns in the grid?
Does this work for a grid of any size?

(c) You will know that a number can be divided by two if its *last* digit is even.
You may know that a number can be divided by three if the *sum* of its digits can be divided by three. These 'rules of divisibility' are quick ways of checking the factors of a number and are useful in calculations especially with fractions.

Find out (or invent) rules of divisibility for all factors from 2 to 12, and show how each one works with two or three examples.
The rule for 7 and 11 (which also works for 13) is so complicated that it is given here – perhaps you can find a better one!

Rule of divisibility for 7, 11 and 13
Split the number into groups of three digits from the right; add the 1st, 3rd, 5th group, etc.; subtract the 2nd, 4th, 6th group, etc.; if the answer is divisible by 7, 11 or 13, then so was the original number.

EXAMPLE
1 458 352 903 becomes 1/458/352/903
   903 + 458 − 352 − 1 = 1008
which *is* divisible by 7.
Therefore 1 458 352 903 is divisible by 7.

(d) Before the days of calculators, a common method of checking addition and multiplication sums was 'casting out nines'.
Each number in a sum is 'reduced' by adding its digits and then subtracting nines until a single-digit remainder is left.
For addition, add the reduced numbers of a sum and reduce their total again. The answer must be the same as the reduced number of the sum's total.
For multiplication, multiply the reduced numbers of a sum and reduce their total again. The answer must be the same as the reduced number of the sum's product.

EXAMPLES

$$\left.\begin{array}{r} 2491 \to 7 \\ 387 \to 0 \\ +\ 25 \to 7 \\ 451 \to 1 \end{array}\right\} \to 6$$

$$3354 \to 6$$

$$\left.\begin{array}{r} 372 \to 3 \\ \times\ 58 \to 4 \end{array}\right\} \to 3$$

$$21576 \to 3$$

Investigate this method with several more examples.

(e) A more reliable alternative to the last method is 'casting out elevens'.
Each number is reduced by adding *alternate* digits, starting with the units, then subtracting the other digits; then subtract elevens until a 'remainder' less than eleven is left.

For addition, the sum of the remainders must equal the remainder of the sum.

For multiplication, the product of the remainders equals the remainder of the product.

Investigate this method with several examples. Neither method is completely reliable – some errors will not be detected. Investigate this by deliberately making errors in your examples.
What kind of error is *not* detected? Why is method **(e)** *more* reliable than method **(d)**?

(f) Finally, here is a strange number puzzle.
Choose any three-digit number, not palindromic, with units and hundreds different by at least two. Reverse the digits, and subtract the smaller number from the larger.
Reverse the digits again, and add.

EXAMPLE

$$\begin{array}{r} 853 \\ 358 \\ \hline 495 \\ 594 \\ \hline 1089 \end{array}$$

What answer do *you* get?

Repeat the puzzle with several different examples.

▲ PROJECT 2

In the last project there were several interesting numerical results. Choose one or two of them that you particularly liked, and try to explain with mathematics why they work out as they do.

EXAMPLE
Investigation **(b)** – a grid with six columns, a square of side three. The square could be anywhere in the grid, so call the first number a. So b must be $a + 2$, c must be $a + (6 \times 2)$, and d is $c + 2$.
Therefore
$$bc - ad = (a + 2)(a + 12) - a(a + 14)$$
which simplifies to
$$a^2 + 14a + 24 - a^2 - 14a = 24$$

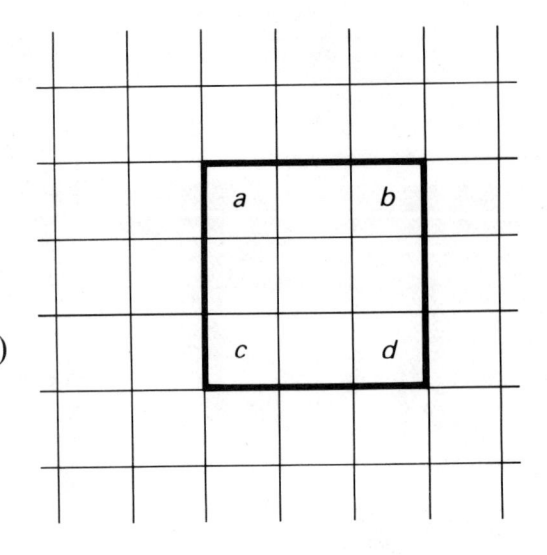

What is the relationship between this number, the number of columns and the size of the square?
Notice that the result means that *any* square of side three in this grid will give the result 24 – it does not depend on the value of a.
Can you find a way of predicting the result for *any* number of columns and *any* size of square?

Useful hints for other investigations:
(i)   a number *abcde* has the value
      $10\,000a + 1000b + 100c + 10d + e$ or...
      $9999a + a + 999b + b + 99c + c + 9d + d + e$
(ii) $7 \times 11 \times 13 = 1001$!

Squares and cubes and... 16

▲ PROJECT 1
Study the diagram below carefully. It shows how geometry can be used to prove an algebraic result.

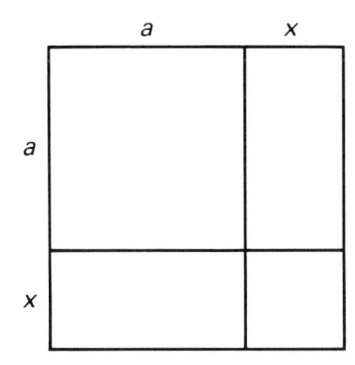

Area of large square = $(a + x)^2$
Areas within large square = $a^2 + ax + ax + x^2$
Therefore
$$(a + x)^2 = a^2 + 2ax + x^2$$

These proofs are often very helpful to younger pupils who might be less familiar with algebra.

(a) Use the diagram below to prove the expansion of $(a - x)^2$.

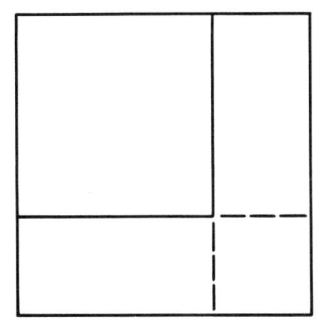

(b) Devise your own proof along similar lines for 'the difference of two squares' result.

■ PROJECT 2
A cube of side $(a + b)$ can be divided into two smaller cubes and six cuboids. Study the diagram carefully. Work out the volumes of the smaller cubes and cuboids, and thus find an expression for the expansion of $(a + b)^3$.

The binomial cube

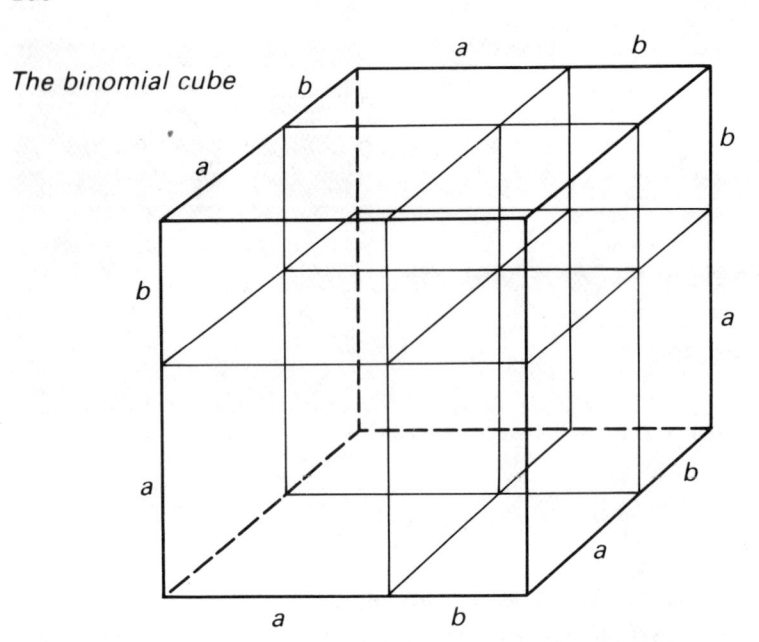

Choose some convenient values for a and b. Construct a cube, open at the top, with sides $(a + b)$. Then construct eight cuboids to fit inside it as shown above. Such a model would be an invaluable classroom exhibit!

Now investigate how similar methods may be used to prove the factorisation of:
(a) $a^3 - b^3$
(**Hint** You need a cube of side a containing four cuboids.)
(b) $a^3 + b^3$
(**Hint** Again you need five cuboids, but not within a cube this time.)

■ PROJECT 3

The ideas in the last section are going to be taken further now, to help you understand the expansion of expressions like $(a + b)^4$ and higher powers.
Of course, geometric models will not be much use as no-one can construct a model with more than three dimensions! But everyday objects can still be used to help solve the problem.
(a) First, take three different books (or different coloured counters, etc.). Suppose you were allowed

to choose only two of them: how many choices have you got?

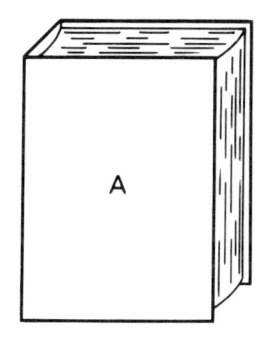

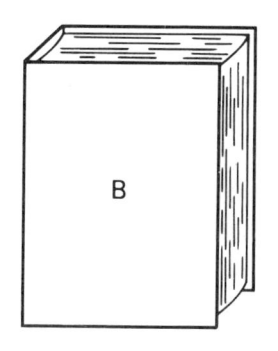

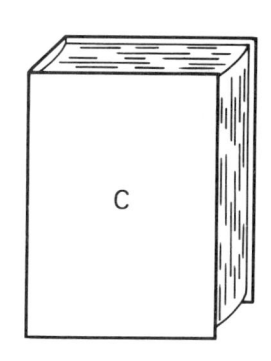

You could choose A + B, or A + C, or B + C (the order doesn't matter) i.e. a total of three choices. How many choices have you got if you're allowed only one book? And if you're allowed three books?

Now take another different book or counter so that you have four to choose from. How many choices have you got each time if you're allowed one, two, three and four of them?
Repeat this investigation for five and six books, and summarise your results in a table as shown.

Number of choices

Take From	1	2	3	4	5	6
3	3	3	1	–	–	–
4	4			1	–	–
5						–
6						

When the table is complete, study the numbers carefully and see if you can recognise any patterns and relationships.

Can you use the table to *predict* how many choices you would have from seven books or more?

This table could be extended indefinitely to calculate the choices from any number of books, but this would clearly be rather tedious.
Can you devise a way of predicting the numbers without using the table?

(b) Now, what has the last section to do with the original problem of expanding $(a + b)^4$?
First, consider the simpler problem of expanding $(a + b)^3$, the result of which was found in Project 2. The problem can be stated as
$$(a + b)(a + b)(a + b)$$
and the expansion clearly must contain some a^3 terms, some a^2b terms, some ab^2 terms and some b^3 terms. But how many of each?

Consider a^3
This term can only be obtained by choosing a from each bracket and multiplying them together.
How many ways are there of choosing three a's from three brackets? (How many ways were there of choosing three books from three available?)

Consider a^2b
This term can be obtained by choosing two a's from the three available, and multiplying them by b from the remaining bracket.
How many ways are there of choosing two a's from three brackets? (How many ways were there of choosing two books from three available?)

How many ways are there of choosing ab^2? And of choosing b^3?
What, then, is the expansion of $(a + b)^3$, and how is it related to your summary table?

Now find the expansions of $(a + b)^4$, $(a + b)^5$ and $(a + b)^6$ ....

Going off at a tangent! 17

PROJECT 1

In this project you will investigate new ways of solving equations. As a first example, consider the quadratic
$$x^2 - 3x - 1 = 0$$
You will know that it could be solved using the quadratic formula, and you may use this to check your results. First, plot the graph of this function for the range shown, using as large a scale as possible.

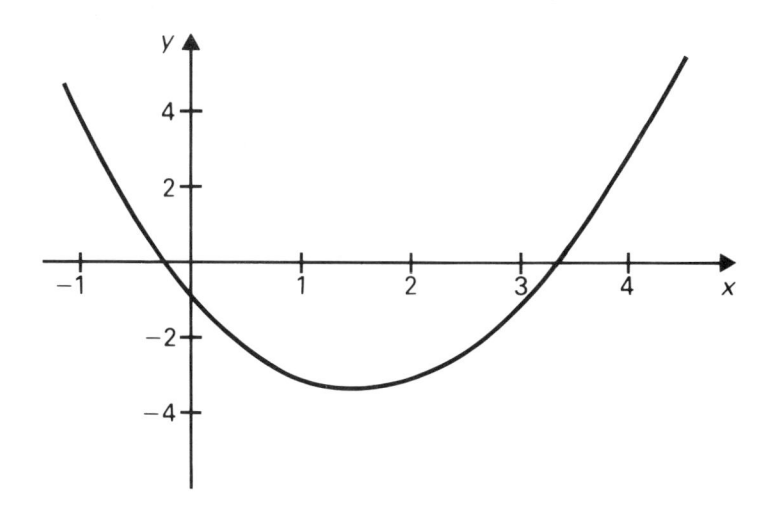

Clearly, one of the solutions lies between $x = 3$ and $x = 4$, and this is the one you are going to find.

(a) Check that when $x = 3$, $y < 0$ (the graph is below the x-axis) and that when $x = 4$, $y > 0$ (the graph is above the x-axis).

Now confirm that when $x = 3.5$, half way between the previous estimates, $y > 0$. Since the graph is above the axis here, but below it at $x = 3$, the solution must be between 3 and 3.5.

Bisect the interval between these two estimates and work out y when $x = 3.25$.

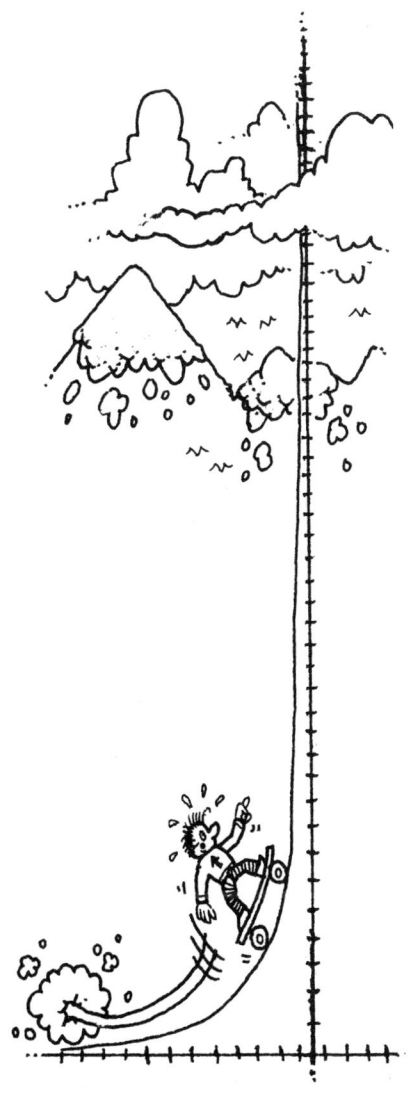

Continue in this way, each time bisecting the interval between estimates either side of the solution until you have confirmed that the solution is 3.303, to three decimal places.
How many 'bisections' did you have to make?

Investigate this technique with other quadractics until you are familiar with it, and then try it with the following equations (for which there is no formula to check with!).

$x^3 + x - 11 = 0$ (a solution between 2 and 3)
$x^3 - 6x + 3 = 0$ (a solution between -2 and -3)
$x^3 - 5x + 3 = 0$ (a solution between 1 and 2).

(b) The sketch below shows part of the previous diagram, near the solution. AP is the ordinate at $(4,0)$ whose height is 3 units. BP is the tangent to the curve at P. Using a large scale, draw this part of the graph as accurately as you can, including the tangent.
Clearly, B is a better estimate of the solution than A was.

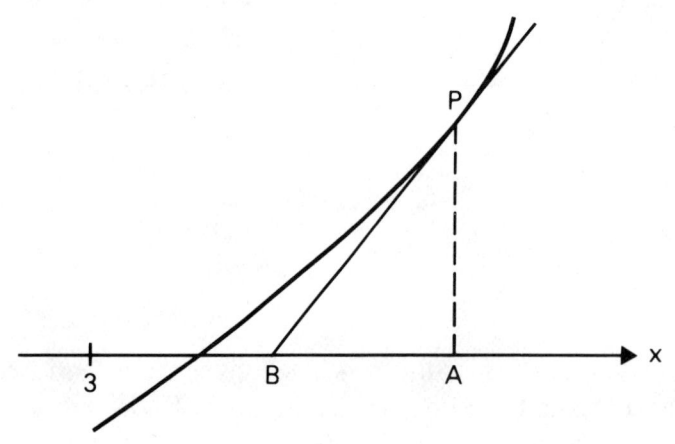

The gradient of BP is $\frac{dy}{dx}$, or $2x - 3$ at $x = 4$, which is $+5$. But the gradient is also equal to $AP \div BA$, or $3 \div (4 - B)$.
So, $5 = 3 \div (4 - B)$, which yields $B = 3.4$.
Check how accurate your graph was!

Now repeat this process drawing an ordinate at B to meet the curve at Q, and a tangent at Q to meet the x-axis at C.

Calculate y and $\frac{dy}{dx}$, when $x = 3.4$, then work out

$$\frac{dy}{dx}(\text{at } x = 3.4) = \frac{y\,(\text{at } x = 3.4)}{3.4 - C}$$

You should find that $C = 3.305$, to three decimal places.

This is very close indeed to the solution, and only a few quite simple calculations were needed.

Moreover, this degree of accuracy could *not* be achieved with a graph.

Use this technique to find the other solution for this equation, taking $x = 0$ as your first estimate. Again, you should find the solution quite quickly.

In general, if A is a first estimate for a solution, then

$$\frac{dy}{dx} \text{ at } A = \frac{y \text{ at } A}{A - B} \quad \text{and } B \text{ is a better estimate.}$$

This is called the **Newton–Raphson iteration method**. Investigate its use further with other quadratics, then try it with the cubic equations given earlier, using the lower of the numbers given as your first estimate.

When you are familiar with the method, try the last equation in **(a)** ($x^3 - 5x + 3 = 0$) again using (a) 1.2 (b) 1.22 (c) 1.23 as your first estimates. Can you explain the very surprising results?

For the determined puzzler

18

This project shows how to devise some quite difficult maths and logic puzzles, which could be collected with those of Investigation 1.

▲ **PROJECT 1: THE FRENCH CODE CROSSWORD**

This is similar to the earlier 'French crossword puzzle' in Investigation 1 except that there may be a number of possible arrangements of the answers. However, there is only one arrangement which yields a particular codeword, and the task is to find that word. (This form of the puzzle is not successful using numbers.)

First, draw a grid (not too large), decide on a codeword and mark a position for it in the grid.

Now write as many words as you can into the grid so that they all fit with each other and with the codeword. (When you write horizontal words, take care that they also form words vertically.) Finally, blank out any empty squares, and make a list of all the words in your grid except the codeword. The puzzler receives just this list with a blank copy of the grid.

List
has
long
he
do
diode, etc.

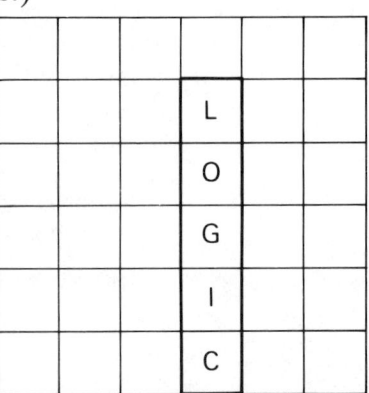

▲ PROJECT 2: MORE AMAZING NUMBERS

This is a very baffling puzzle, not too hard to set. The puzzler is presented with a grid full of numbers between, say, 0 and 100 (which only appear once each). He must find a path from the 0 to the 100, but
(i) must only move horizontally or vertically,
(ii) must not go over any number twice, and
(iii) must always move to a *higher* number.

8	7	4			41	42	47
10		3		40		50	
11		0	35	38		55	
16			34		70	59	
17	21	22	29	33		72	
						73	80
				100		82	
				97	90	84	

The larger the grid the better, but start off with one about eight square.
Mark a 0 and a 100, and a twisting pathway of numbers between them (each larger than the one before) as shown.
Count how many moves there are along this pathway, to give as a clue, and make a copy of the grid so far as the solution.

Now write a number into each of the remaining squares, attempting to lay 'false trails' – paths of numbers that increase for some distance but then come to a dead end i.e. to a point where there are only smaller numbers in every direction.
Start filling in the grid around the area of the 0, taking care not to provide 'short cuts'!

▲ PROJECT 3: MASTERMIND

In this puzzle there is a word or number to be discovered. Several other words or numbers of the same length are given as clues, along with information about how many letters or digits of these are the same as those of the word or number to be found.

EXAMPLES

1

S	L	A	V	E	3
A	L	E	R	T	2
T	R	I	B	E	2
S	T	A	R	E	1
T	R	A	I	T	0

2

			✓	✗
2	5	1	2	0
3	1	0	1	1
3	2	4	1	0
6	4	0	0	0

1 A five-letter word is to be found. It contains three letters of the word 'slave', in the same positions as they appear in 'slave'. It contains two letters of the word 'alert' in the same positions, etc.
Considerable care must be taken in setting these clues. Every letter of the target word must be referred to at least once among the clues. There should be a clue which contains several letters the same as the target word, and a clue which contains none of the same letters; however, this last clue must contain some letters in common with the other clues, to help the puzzler with elimination.

2 This is an alternative form of the puzzle, not only because there is a number to be found and the clues are therefore numbers, but also because more information is given.
The column marked '✓' shows how many digits of the clue are the same as the target number and in the same position. The column marked '✗' shows how many of the other digits in the clue also appear in the target number but in different positions.
Again, there should be a clue which is quite similar to the target, and one which contains none of the same digits but which does have digits in common with the other clues.

It can be quite difficult to devise clues for these puzzles so that on the one hand there are not too many clues and the puzzle is quite hard, but on the other hand there are just enough clues for the puzzle to be solvable!

■ PROJECT 4

Example 2 can also be used as a code for secret messages which is very hard to break.

A puzzle is set as before but using numbers 1 – 25, thus it is a string of numbers which is to be discovered. A string of *five* numbers would refer to a *five*-letter word in the message.

Having decided the string to be found, you devise a letter grid as shown below; each number in the string corresponds to a position in this grid, reading from left to right and top to bottom. In the position corresponding to the first number of the string, you write the first letter of the word to be coded. Continue until all five letters have been filled in, then write other letters at random in the empty spaces.

EXAMPLE
The message:

1	6	2	10	5	3
4	6	2	13	5	3
4	14	8	13	6	2
2	6	2	13	6	2
4	6	8	4	6	0

Solving this as before yields the string: 1, 14, 2, 13, 5

The key:

G	E	B	L	T
N	Y	Q	I	W
U	F	A	R	O
J	K	P	V	D
C	X	H	M	S

Position 1 is 'G', position 14 is 'R', and so on.
The coded word is GREAT.

■ PROJECT 5: THE FREQUENCY CROSSWORD

In this crossword the clues are given by numbers written into the grid, each number always replacing the same letter.

As a further clue, the frequency with which some of the letters appear can be given.

The puzzle is better if there are not too many words, and if all the words have a common theme.

First draw a grid and write in several words, say, to do with mathematics. Then beside each letter write a number, always the same number for the same letter.

Count how many times each letter appears in the puzzle.

Finally, write the grid out again including the numbers but not the letters.

Frequency clues

e = 7
i and t = 4
r = 3
a, n, c and m = 2
no other letter has a frequency more than 1.

1 e	2 s	3 t	4 i	5 m	6 a	3 t	1 e
	7 u					1 e	
	8 b			9 r	4 i	10 n	11 g
	3 t						
12 p	9 r	4 i	5 m	1 e		1 e	
	6 a		13 o			14 v	
	15 c	4 i	9 r	15 c	16 l	1 e	
	3 t		1 e			10 n	

PROJECT 6: ELIMINATION

This a very popular kind of puzzle, quite difficult both to devise and to solve. The puzzler has to deduce the characteristics that belong to each of a group of people, but using only a few obscure clues – a kind of detective investigation. Usually, a 'truth-table' grid is provided to help with the elimination of possibilities.

First, devise the situation. In this example there are four schoolchildren, and the information about them consists of name, hair, age and favourite sport.

Adam	blond	15	hockey
Beryl	black	16	tennis
Chris	red	14	snooker
Diana	brown	13	badminton

Note that *all* the characteristics are different, and they should not be too obvious – these sports were chosen because generally they are played by both sexes.

The truth-table grid must be set out carefully so that any characteristic can be matched against each of the others.

If, as in the example here, there are four characteristics (say, A, B, C and D) then the grid should be set out thus:

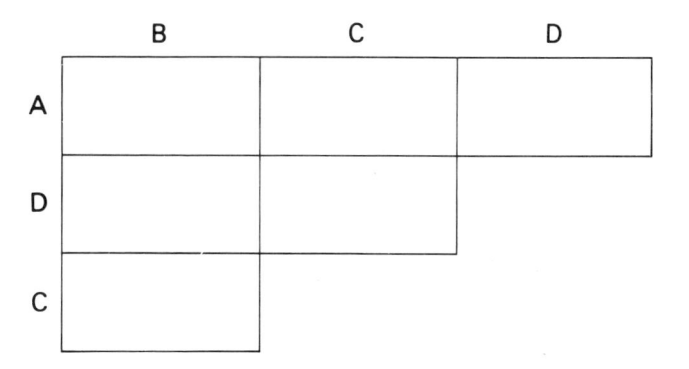

The actual grid for this example is shown overleaf. Note that the order of the characteristics has been mixed up so as not to give any extra clues.

You will need a copy of the grid yourself, to use in devising the clues, as well as a copy for the puzzler.

	brown	red	black	blond	13	14	16	15	badminton	hockey	snooker	tennis
Adam												
Beryl												
Chris												
Diana												
hockey												
badminton												
tennis												
snooker												
15												
14												
16												
13												

The most difficult part is now to devise just enough clues for the puzzle to be solvable, and no more. To help with this you need a copy of the truth-table grid which you will fill in as you think up the clues, in just the same way as the puzzler would. (The difference, of course, is that you know the answers!)

How to use the grid
Suppose the first clue you think up is:
'Adam, who is two years older than the badminton player, has blond hair.'

What are the logical consequences of this statement?

>Adam *is* blond, is *not* brown-, red- or black-haired.
>Adam *must* be 15 or 16, so *cannot* be ...
>Adam does *not* play ...
>The badminton player *is* 13 or ...., and *not* ... or ...
>The badminton player is *not* blond.
>Beryl, Chris and Diana are *not* ...

Suppose the next clue is to be:
'The oldest of the children has black hair and plays tennis.'

The logical consequences of this statement are:

> The 16-year-old *has* black hair, is *not* ...
> The 16-year-old *plays* ..., *not* ...
> (Alternatively, the tennis player *is* ..., *not* ...)

Putting the two clues so far together, we can also deduce that:

> Adam is *not* 16, so Adam *is* ...
> Adam does *not* play ...
> *Neither* the 13- nor the 14-year-old play ...

Now study your copy of the grid below and see how the information so far has been entered.

'✓' means yes, and '✗' means no.

	brown	red	black	blond	13	14	16	15	badminton	hockey	snooker	tennis
Adam	✗	✗	✗	✓	✗	✗	✗	✓	✗			✗
Beryl				✗				✗				
Chris				✗				✗				
Diana				✗				✗				
hockey			✗				✗					
badminton			✗	✗			✗	✗				
tennis	✗	✗	✓	✗	✗	✗	✓	✗				
snooker			✗				✗					
15	✗	✗	✗	✓								
14			✗	✗								
16	✗	✗	✓	✗								
13			✗	✗								

Note that a great deal *can* be deduced from just the first two clues, and a large proportion of the grid completed. The task now is to devise further clues concerning the blank spaces that still remain.

Check your own deductions carefully as you go until the grid is complete: one '√' and 3 '×'s for hair, age and sport in each of the first four rows (names).

PROJECT 7: THE NEIGHBOUR CODE

This last puzzle is easy to set but quite infuriatingly hard to solve!

It consists of a grid of squares, each square containing a letter and a number.
Some of the letters, when correctly arranged, form a coded word – the other letters are decoys.
The number is a clue to how many of the squares in the set consisting of its own square and its horizontal or vertical neighbours contain letters of the codeword.

EXAMPLE
The codeword in this grid contains five letters.

M	A	H	E
0	1	2	3
R	T	I	L
0	1	2	2
H	L	S	Z
1	1	1	2
E	T	W	O
0	1	1	1

| ┌─────┐ |
| M | means none of the letters M, A or R are included;
| ___0_| |

|┌─────┐|
|A | means one of the letters A, M, H or T is included;
|___1_| |

|┌─────┐|
|H | means two of the letters H, A, E or I are included,
|___2_| and so on.

In this way certain letters can be eliminated entirely from the search. Then it's down to logic and trial and error!

Make a copy of the example and check it through for yourself so that you understand how it works.

To devise the puzzle, follow these steps:
- choose a codeword, not too many letters;
- make a grid with at least twice as many squares as there are letters in the codeword;
- insert the letters of the codeword into the grid, one to a square, but position them carefully. There should be blocks of the grid containing *no* letters of the codeword so that some squares will contain a number zero (to help the puzzler);
- write other random letters into the empty squares;
- now check carefully through the grid, one square at a time, counting how many of the letters of the codeword are contained either in that square or its horizontal or vertical neighbours. Write this number into the square.

For a more difficult puzzle, diagonal neighbours may be included in the counting.

Here is an example of this sort for you to practise on!

I	U	R	B	H
1	2	1	1	0
T	D	G	P	M
2	3	1	1	0
C	W	Y	A	K
1	2	1	2	1
E	S	A	V	O
1	1	1	2	2
N	F	P	L	E
0	0	1	2	2

115